YEMEN

INVITATION TO A VOYAGE IN ARABIA FELIX

JACQUES HÉBERT

Photographs by Marc Hébert

YEMEN

INVITATION TO A VOYAGE IN ARABIA FELIX

Preface by Yusuf M. Abdallah

Translation by Alan Brown

HERITAGE PUBLISHING
MONTREAL

Cover design: ADAM DESIGN
Color separations and stripping: StanMont

End papers: Sana'a at dawn
Cover photo: Stained-glass window of a mafraj in Taiz.

© 1989 AZAL PUBLISHING
All rights reserved

ISBN 2-9801500-1-0

© 1989 HERITAGE PUBLISHING
All rights reserved
Bibliothèque nationale du Québec
Legal deposit—2th quarter 1989

ISBN 2-7625-5996-0

CONTENTS

To Alex and Gérard Pelletier, true friends with whom I have shared my joys and sorrows over forty years.

This time, the joys of Yemen...

PREFACE

An experienced Arab traveller, many centuries ago, came to the conclusion that travel is a good habit, and, in order to convey this conviction to others, he composed two elegant verses, summarizing his opinion on the usefulness of travel. He said:

"Travel! Travel, my friend, and five precious *benefits* are awaiting you:
Recreating the soul, earning one's living, acquiring knowledge, appreciating others' culture and winning the friendship of a good companion."

If the reader may allow me to add one more relevant verse, which was spoken also many centuries ago in Arabia, then certainly he will get the message of this extraordinary guide book and will accept the invitation of its highly experienced author, in both travelling and writing. The verse says:

"Sana'a is an indispensable goal to those who love travel,
No matter how long it takes them to reach it,
No matter how many camels to ride."

In his book, Senator Jacques Hébert is both a poet and an objective, demanding traveller. He advocates travel but at the same time "benefits" of travel are not obtained everywhere. He yearns and searches for what is behind the stars. He admires the good and the genuine and refuses the superficial and the inconsistent.

One may not share some of his allegorical impressions or may disagree with some of his critical views, but certainly the reader will admire his love of beauty, art and the heritage of mankind. As a Yemeni, who had the chance to read so many books on Yemen, some of which have now become "classics", I proclaim that I found this book different. It is daring, adventurous and spontaneous. Afar, beyond the oceans, more than 15,000 km away, one discovers a friend of Yemen who could grasp the reality of things and present it to others intelligently and attractively. *Invitation to a voyage in Arabia Felix* is more than a guide book and it is more than a detailed interpretation of the Arab traveller's verses chanted many centuries ago. In Yemen, the past still lives on and the invitation still holds good.

Dr. Yusuf M. ABDALLAH
Vice-president of General
Organisation of
Antiquities and Libraries
Sanaa

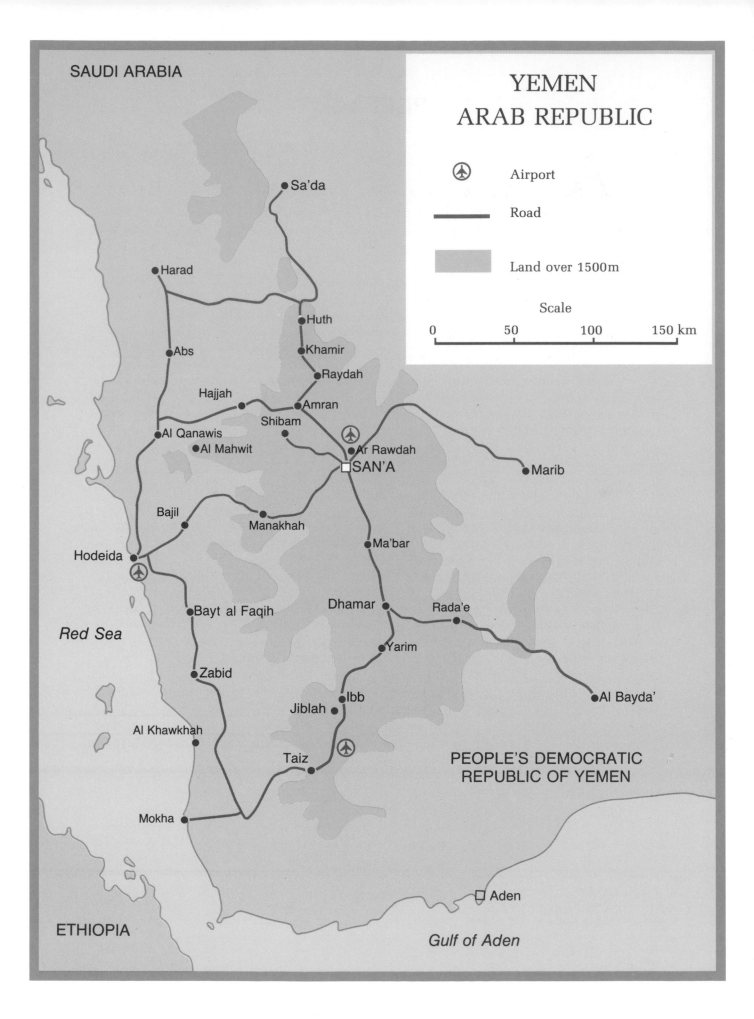

FOREWORD

Travel is fatal to prejudice, bigotry and narrow-mindedness.

Mark Twain

I wonder if there are many people in the world who have not, however briefly, dreamed of one day seeing Yemen?

My private image of this country has fascinated me ever since I was a child, a time when Yemen still lived withdrawn in its mystery, closed off from foreign influences. After the 1962 revolution which ended the long reign of the imams, Yemen sought to shake off the constraints imposed by a unique, rich civilization that had survived for three thousand years but had more in common with Biblical days than with our Star-Wars era. Romantics like myself catch themselves regretting the upheavals that deprive mankind of the last vestiges of paradise on earth— those fragments of Eden where we still find traces of an original grace and innocence.

Yes, an armchair romantic I was indeed, for prior to 1962 Yemen, under the tyrannical imams, was no paradise for liberty; nor for women, excluded from schooling and forced to till the fields; nor for children, who died too young. So much for original grace and innocence! But we must look, instead, at how beautiful this country is today, at once young and old, flowering at last after a long germination, like a desert plant that brings forth its rarest blooms after a sudden rain.

In this book I want to deal only with North Yemen, that is, the Yemen Arab Republic... but how can we ignore the existence of South Yemen (the People's Democratic Republic of Yemen)? The two countries have so much in common that they should, by rights, form but a single state. Until the end of the last century historians gave the name of Yemen to the vast province in the south of the Arabian peninsula, or Greater Yemen, which, incidentally, the ancient authors had baptized "Happy Arabia" (*Arabia Felix*). It was the presence of the British in Aden, from 1839 onward, and their domination of the southern tribes, that created an artificial frontier which still exists today. But to simplify matters, I will use the word Yemen throughout this book to designate North Yemen. But, some day, I will tell the fascinating story of South Yemen...

No book is objective. It can only, at a given moment, be the vision of an individual with all his prejudices, who sees some things clearly and others darkly. In my case the problem is aggravated by the fact that I'm in love with Yemen! As soon as I set foot in this fabulous country it was love at first sight. I have been there three times, for short periods, but I knew at once that even if I spent the rest of my life there I would never weary of it. What I'm offering you, then, is not an objective accounting but, quite simply, a love story!

CHAPTER I

SANA'A, MARIB AND THE ANCIENT KINGDOMS

Understanding the world—this is already comparable to the stable and uncontested wealth of a great landowner. But making a discovery is so much more—a sudden flood of riches, the stroke of fortune that doubles a man's capital when he stumbles on some treasure as on an inspiration.

Georges Duhamel

In Paris, eight hours' flying time still separate us from Sana'a, the beautiful capital of Yemen. We land there around midnight.

In the pitch dark, the headlights of the car our Yemenite friends have provided give kaleidoscopic glimpses of strange facades, eucalyptus trees shuddering a fine dust from their leaves, a few turbaned passers-by (night-hawks, nebulous, ghostly), and barking dogs.

As always when I arrive in a new country, an extraordinary well-being overwhelms me. I become like a child again, fascinated by the slightest sound, a new fragrance, a breeze, an unaccustomed gesture, a murmur in the dark.

This world is an immense, mad castle, like Ludwig of Bavaria's folly in stone, replete with towers and turrets, with minuscule, delightful rooms, "ornate ceilings"*, "deep mirrors", cellars and dungeons, endless corridors

---

* Quotes in this paragraph are translated from Baudelaire's poem *Invitation au voyage* which suggested the sub-title of this book.

← Young and proud to be a Yemenite.   The Bab al Yaman gate in Sana'a. →

11

that may, perhaps, lead to yet another secret room where huge windows look out on "this country which resembles you" with its reign of "luxury, calm, delight".

Tonight, I softly open the gate of Yemen.

Sana'a, the capital, with 427,000 inhabitants, is a precious jewel set in a ring of mountains with an altitude of 2,300 metres. In the gold light of morning, viewing it from my hotel window, I was stunned by the architectural beauty of this amazing city, which may be the oldest still-inhabited city on earth; and by its secret gardens surrounded by earthen walls; and by its innumerable minarets rising in a random pattern.

Unlike so many other beautiful old Arab cities, such as Baghdad or Cairo, Sana'a has not been spoiled by the invasion of concrete and of modern buildings. It has preserved all its millenary beauty, and even houses that have been built more recently (not as high as the old ones) use traditional materials and respect the basic characteristics of the Yemenite style. Oddly, however, in the new neighbourhoods, the doors of garages, courtyards and shops are in heavy sheet metal decorated by wrought iron and painted all in the same colour: sky blue!

Of all the cities I know, none resembles Sana'a, and none, by far, can be compared with it. So it is with real delight that I plunge into my exploration, willingly succumbing to its unreal beauty, admiring its earthen ramparts from which it has spilled out in all directions, and its extraordinary stone houses five or six storeys high, with big arched windows of coloured glass which cause the light to dance in palaces as in more humble homes. Held in place by plaster mouldings, the pieces of glass form geometric patterns.

These old houses are all dissimilar, with their facades of brick and hewn stone (gray, pink, black or green, fitted without mortar, never arranged twice in the same way). Even the bricks are patterned or placed to create a play of light and shadow. To enliven gray or ochre surfaces, geometric motifs in plaster surround the windows, and whitewashed cornices gleam like diadems.

Arab houses normally have bare walls and few windows, the decorator's best efforts being saved for the interior courtyard, where the family gathers, perhaps around a fountain. In Yemen these characteristics are to be found

An architectural gem: house in Sana'a. →

14

only in the tropical Tihama region. More openly, the Yemenite house rises against the sky, proud and intrepid as a medieval castle, its immense windows looking out on the world, some with projecting open-work bays in brick, called *shubbaks*, or the larger *kushks* with wooden lattices or turned wooden posts set around. Safe from the eyes of the curious, the women come here for fresh air or a glimpse of life in the street—or to see who is knocking at their own door. These well-ventilated appendages also serve as storage space for food.

The ground floor, six metres high or more, is always built of hewn stone, while the upper floors are faced with brick. It is pierced by tiny windows and provides room for the animals (goats, donkeys, dromedaries) and for storage of rice, wheat, sorghum and oil.

The only touch of glory on the ground floor is its great wooden door, often decorated with large metal studs and an elaborate knocker. The door is sometimes crowned by an ancient lintel with ornate arabesques or even inscriptions in Sabaean, a pre-Islamic script.

The door opens into a vestibule leading to a stone staircase. The second storey, at least three metres high, contains a communal room, bedrooms, a "water-room" or, in the case of wealthy families, a modern bathroom. According to the size of the family there will be three of four more similar floors, and a high terrace where the women hang their wash to dry or relax with the children. The kitchen is always on the upper floors and communicates with the terrace and sometimes with the hall of honour or *mafraj*, which is lit by great windows on three sides. Simply furnished with a fine carpet and cushions along the walls, the *mafraj* is the realm of the males of the family.

The four exterior walls and the internal ones dividing the house into two or three are supporting walls that bear rough-squared tree trunks on which the wooden floors are laid. Walls, ceilings and visible beams are plastered, always in white. Sometimes in the *mafraj* the plaster is sculptured.

In the old town, through a labyrinth of narrow, congested streets that recall the *souks* of Fez, we go from shop to shop, wide-eyed as children: Minuscule stands, sometimes no more than an alcove in the stone wall where a lone craftsman lovingly polishes *jambia* blades, the large, curved daggers most Yemenite males wear stuck amidships in their wide sashes. Every inch

Wooden *kushk* in Sana'a. →

16

of the street is a poem: here the broad sashes embroidered in gold thread; there, raisins and nuts; or a small jewelers' area where handsome necklaces of gold or silver filigree are sold *by their weight*; and a display of spices where strong fragrances can turn your head. A motley, exuberant crowd jostles past the shops, discussing, haggling, perhaps bantering with the melon vendor, who ends up serving tea to everyone. Men dominate the street scene as they dominate Yemenite society. Among the triumphant males, discreetly furtive forms slip by: women, often veiled and so swaddled as to be shapeless. Yet for a brief moment, from the fold of the veil two immense dark eyes underlined with kohl flash in the sunlight.

But the street, what a show! Two musicians sit on the ground and start beating tambourines. Immediately a crowd gathers—men only—and three Yemenites perform a traditional dance, brandishing their daggers at arm's length. When they are exhausted, three others replace them. Will it go on forever?

No doubt one can walk alone in perfect safety in Old Sana'a, through the forty *souks* with their seventeen hundred shops, discovering a thousand surprises, but in this tangled maze it is prudent to take along a guide to show us things that we would otherwise have missed. He will facilitate the task of the amateur photographer, find the best bargains or decipher an Arabic inscription on a wormeaten wooden lintel. My guide spoke fluent English, French and Italian... and knew absolutely everyone in the city!

For example, it was thanks to Faisal that I ventured into a narrow passage that opened on the ruins of the oldest well in Sana'a. He showed me the path worn by the dromedary that marched to and fro to raise the water and fill the basin where the women came to fetch it. Nearby was an unexpected garden where flowers and vegetables flourished under the palms. It belonged to the nearest mosque, a fine grouping of white cupolas built by the Turks.

We pass in front of a cinema where an Indian film is playing. A few steps farther on I am intrigued by a large metal locker with a padlock. Without Faisal I would never have known what this strange cabinet was used for. "It's for checking *jambias*," he explained. Yemenites are not allowed to take their precious dagger into the movie theatre. They have to check it for the sum of five riyals, and claim their own as they leave the show.

Jambia dancer in a Sana'a market. →

18

At every corner there's something astonishing or admirable. Here are two old men kneeling towards Mecca to pray. There, sitting on the ground, a group of children are playing *amra* with pebbles. Farther on an old, bearded singer dances and sings to the accompaniment of his tambourine.

A long walk in the Bab-el-Yemen market. A string of tiny shops where a merchant has barely room to squat behind his baskets of raisins or coffee-husks used for making *qishr*, a drink more prized than coffee itself. Craftsmen work away in their cramped spaces, grouped by trades: *jambia* makers, makers of *jambia* sashes, *jambia* sharpeners. A shoemaker has set up business in the street: while his customers wait barefoot, he repairs their shoes, and when business is slack he carves sandals out of fine leather. There are two craftsmen making cushions for *mafrajs*. On display stalls, open-air style, stand bottles of imported perfume, transistors, cassettes and assorted plastic articles.

A tarpaulin hangs in a high doorway. "Would you like to see a real caravanserai, several centuries old?" asks Faisal. He lifts the canvas and shows us into an immense hall, a vaulted gallery with massive stone pillars. Here, in the old days, caravans stayed for the night, men and animals.

We visit the Jewish quarter, where Jews are scarce now as a result of the exodus of 1947. "But how can anyone tell?" says Faisal. "They speak Arabic and are just as Yemenite as we are." Here the houses are built with sun-dried bricks covered with a coating of clay mixed with straw. They are one-storey buildings. If there is a second floor, that means it was a recent addition. Yemen was always hospitable to Jews, who were excellent and industrious artisans, but the imams imposed certain restrictions, such as forbidding them to build houses more than one storey high.

One could, one should, spend days in this *souk*, where even the displays of fruits and vegetables are an enchantment: beautiful green grapes, fat watermelons, chubby onions, potatoes, carrots, tomatoes, corn, dates, papayas, bananas, guavas. Farther along are whole-wheat rolls, pyramids of eggs, bunches of *qat* (a plant that is chewed to produce a slight euphoria).

A woman sits in front of a hundred anonymous little pouches. Without Faisal, how could we guess that she is offering us Yemen's most famous products, known for thousands of years: frankincense and myrrh? Just beside her, a gold vendor. Within arm's reach, all that is needed to outfit the Three Wise Men...

Old singer with tambourine. →

20

Occasionally it happens that I simply lose myself alone in the old town, armed with my thorough ignorance, swept along by the moving throng in the dusty streets and the shadowy lanes of the market. I stop in front of a house perhaps a thousand years old to admire its lovely balance, the pattern of the balconies, the scintillating white of the plaster that outlines the doors, windows and cornices on the ochre background of stone or brick. I linger in a shop so small that it can accomodate only one or two customers at a time. A vendor of old jewelry offers me tea and his three words of English. Intricate necklaces, endless earrings, heavy bracelets of tarnished silver, hung from the walls or from the ceiling above the merchant's head, as he sits cross-legged on a rich Persian rug. An ancient hookah completes the décor. In a dark little alcove I spy bunches of *qat* waiting to be chewed at the appropriate time. As we chat, a peasant pushes me discreetly aside so that he can approach the merchant and offer a few family jewels for sale. He opens his handkerchief to show them. After a good quarter-hour of haggling the peasant goes away happy with a handful of riyals, which seems to me slim pickings for two silver bracelets and a pendant set with an agate the colour of wild honey.

"These jewels are not silver," my new friend explains. "It is white metal or bronze with 20 or 30 per cent silver added. See the difference..." And he shows me some pieces very similar as to workmanship but much more expensive, in solid silver. At a very good price I buy a few necklaces (20 or 30 percent silver added) which the merchant assures me are nearly a century old. In this incredible country, anything is possible.

Lunch in the former palace of the last Imam's son. A splendid traditional house converted to a hotel, as a number of other palaces have been. Our host is a political figure, a convinced republican, needless to say, but has a noble bearing with his white-trained turban, his green-sheathed dagger, looking like a prince out of the *Thousand and One Nights*, "... a good prince loved by his people," etc.

At the end of a very tasty Yemenite meal, my host presents me with a beautiful photo album of Yemen. The magic of photography often embellishes reality in such books, making us believe that these exceptional faces, superb monuments, astonishing landscapes and lovely villages are the general rule, while they are, in fact, only exceptional views. Leafing through the album, I can't help telling my host, "These photos are truly magnificent, but the reality of Yemen is more beautiful than a painter, writer or photographer

Traditional house of stone and brick. →

22

can express." It is indeed a country that constantly moves us by the beauty of its scenery and architecture as well as by the purity and pride of its inhabitants, the nobility of their bearing, their sense of human brotherhood, their exquisite courtesy toward foreigners and their ebullient love of life which overflows at all times.

A first stroll in Sana'a's ancient streets awakens in the traveler a desire to dig into the past of a people capable of building a city like this so many centuries ago.

Logically, one should start any stay in Yemen by a visit to Marib and other sites where vestiges can be found of pre-Islamic history, which is still largely unknown to outsiders and even to the Yemenites themselves. If Yemen is so different from the other countries of the Arabian Peninsula, it is precisely because its cultural roots go deeper, and the proud pre-Islamic kingdoms left their permanent mark on the personality of the Yemenites, long-civilized.

The strong impact of Islam, which came opportunely to nourish the spiritual and temporal aspirations of the Yemenites, no doubt contributed to a certain forgetfulness of the past, as the devouring fire of Christianity almost destroyed the last vestiges of Graeco-Roman culture. But in Yemen as elsewhere—God be praised!—there survived a certain will to safeguard a heritage which now contributes to the collective pride of both northern and southern Yemenites.

In the care of Abdullah, a crafty old driver, I leave in search of Marib. Abdullah is a good driver, but he has his idiosyncrasies. For example, as he had no time for a breakfast before we left, he eats it while driving at 100 kilometres per hour. With his left hand he holds a glass of hot tea, his left forearm leaning on the steering wheel. With his right hand he fumbles in a bag, breaking off a piece of the unleavened bread that constitutes his main course. Luckily, at this early hour there is little traffic.

Like most parts of Yemen, this landscape is at once grandiose, sublime and rugged. The lack of rain on the plateau where we're driving has discouraged all growth except a few rare vineyards. High mountains lie all around us, stretched out in the heavy morning mist like giants in eiderdown.

After 25 kilometres we begin the passage of Mount Dhu-Marmar, with its high plateau from which we see in the distance the ruins of a town,

Thousand-year-old well in Sana'a. →

probably close to 2,000 years old. Rugged mountains, arid plateaus where a few thorn trees manage, God knows how, to survive. Gradually the landscape changes, a few palm trees appear, a few dromedaries... and, nearer Marib, slim dunes of sand creeping forward: the desert is here, stretching out its golden claws.

Ten kilometres before we arrive we glimpse the skyline of Marib, like a royal crown poised on the bald cranium of a hill. I imagine travellers a century or two ago, arriving on foot or by dromedary, touched by this impressive spectacle. This old city was once the vibrant capital of a kingdom; now it is an empty shell. A few noble houses are still occupied, but most of them are falling in ruins. Here and there among the rubble one finds a stone inscribed in the handsome characters of the Sabaean script, that of Yemen's pre-Islamic past and now supplanted by Arabic.

Some distance from here a new Marib has been built using much concrete and asphalt and many electric cables. This seems to us uninspired, but what will travellers say who see the place three hundred years from now?

In the meantime, we go to visit the ruins of the famous Marib dam, built, it is believed, in the 8th century before Christ, to catch the flood waters of the streams from the high plateaus. Thanks to the water collected in this basin (700 meters long, 18 high and 60 wide at the base) the whole region around Marib became extremely fertile until the dam was destroyed at the end of the pre-Islamic era. It is almost unbelievable that this immense dike of earth and stones managed to last for more than a thousand years. The Yemenites have built a new dam which should bring fresh life to this beautiful region threatened by the advance of the desert.

We can still admire the five symmetrical columns of what is said to have been the royal palace of the Queen of Sheba. If true, this would explain why the local people refer to it as the "throne of Bilquis" (the Queen's name). According to some archaeologists these pillars survive from a temple. Some distance away rise the eight columns of the temple of Awwam. Or is it a palace as the people of Marib claim? The archeologists say it is a temple.

A mysterious epoch, many of whose secrets remain unknown. What is certain is that in the first millenium B.C. vast kingdoms prospered quietly in this part of the world, contemporary with ancient Egypt, Greece and Rome,

A pillar in the southern sluice of the Marib dam. →

26

whose history is familiar to us. The archeological sites of Marib, Timna, Ma'in, Shabwa, Barakish and the collection of sculptures and bas-reliefs displayed in the National Museum in Sana'a give only a slight notion of the level of civilization in these kingdoms, which played a major role in all the exchanges and trade relations among Asia, the Middle East and Mediterranean Europe thanks to the famous Frankincense Road, the great caravan route of the Yemenites. It may have been to stimulate this trade that the queen of Sheba went to visit king Solomon.

In the Book of Kings it is written: "And when the Queen of Sheba heard of the fame of Solomon concerning the name of the Lord, she came to prove him with hard questions. And she came to Jerusalem with a very great train, with camels that bare spices, and very much gold, and precious stones: and when she was come to Solomon, she communed with him of all that was in her heart. And Solomon told her all her questions: there was not any thing hid from the king, which he told her not... And King Solomon gave unto the Queen of Sheba all her desire, whatsoever she asked, beside that which Solomon gave her of his royal bounty. So she turned and went to her own country, she and her servants."

(I Kings: 1-3, 13.)

As I walked with a heavy, silent tread in the sand of the dunes around Marib, I tried to imagine Bilquis, queen of Sheba, on a richly caparisoned dromedary. Before and behind her, hundreds of other "ships of the desert" bearing the queen's followers, her servants, members of the royal family, and the officers of the army who accompanied her on this perilous voyage away from her kingdom. Besides the royal guard there were thousands of foot-soldiers strung out along the endless caravan of dromedaries loaded with food, baggage and the many presents Queen Bilquis carried to Solomon, no doubt to impress him but also to persuade him of the importance of establishing good relations with such a wealthy kingdom. She brought frankincense, myrrh and gold, but also, out of Asia, pearls, silk and spices, the origin of which queen Bilquis, canny like all Yemenites, would take pains to conceal.

Presumably the voyage took place in wintertime, when the desert climate is more or less tolerable, but let's try to imagine the endurance test it was for a young woman to bear the long days when they were on the move, the implacable sun, the sand storms. Mounted on the hump of a dromedary one is constantly tossed this way and that, as if one were riding

Temple ruins in the land of the Queen of Sheba. →

the waves in some frail barque. How many months did it take to travel those several thousand kilometres?

If we believe in legends (and the movies), the lovely queen made a quick recovery from her trials once safely in Solomon's palace. Mischief makers have maintained that Queen Bilquis became more than intimate with the great king of Israel, son of David and Bathsheba, though he had a challenging harem of his own. The emperors of Ethiopia (the last of whom was Haile Selassie) claimed to be descendents of Menelek, the offspring of this union. In 1957, when I met the emperor in his palace in Addis Ababa, the "King of Kings" made a discreet allusion to his illustrious descent. With a trace of a mocking smile and in impeccable French. Was not one of his titles "Lion of Judah"? But the archeologists and historians have their work cut out for them if we insist on irrefutable proof.

Because of its very favourable geographical situation and the dynamism of its inhabitants, Greater Yemen was the most prosperous part of the Arabian Peninsula in the days of the kingdoms, which at first expanded along the valleys in the eastern part of the country.

Marib, capital of the kingdom of Saba, dominated the valley of the Adhanah. The kingdom of Qataban was established in the valley of the Bayhan; that of Hadramaut along the Armah, and, finally, in the rich valley of the Jawf, the Ma'in kingdom had its hour of glory. Three centuries B.C.

A century later, it was the turn of Qataban to impose its law on an immense territory whose agricultural production underwent sensational growth thanks to ingenious irrigation systems.

The kingdom of Hadramaut, the capital of which was Shabwa, exercised its influence on a wide tract of Yemen beginning in the first century B.C.

Though the kingdom of Saba, which extended its dominion as far as Ethiopia, is the cradle of Yemen's history, each of the other kingdoms, over the centuries, succeeded in one part or another of the territory (and to the detriment of its neighbours) in controlling the Frankincense Road, which along with agriculture was the main source of the area's prosperity.

More recently, the kingdom of the Himyarites, with its capital Zafar, became one of the most celebrated, from the beginning of the Christian era

Green grapes for sale. →

to its decline five hundred years later, by virtue of managing to gather under a single crown almost all of the Yemenite kingdoms.

It was mainly because of the trade in frankincense and myrrh that the ancient kingdoms developed such a high level of trade with the Mediterranean countries, consolidating their prosperity and power.

Frankincense, the resinous substance which, when burnt, gives off an unctuous odour, was supposed to possess certain interesting medicinal properties. Temples between Karnak in Egypt, and Nineva in Mesopotamia, used it copiously in their religious ceremonies. Myrrh also had medicinal properties, and was used as a base for making perfume. The gold, frankincense

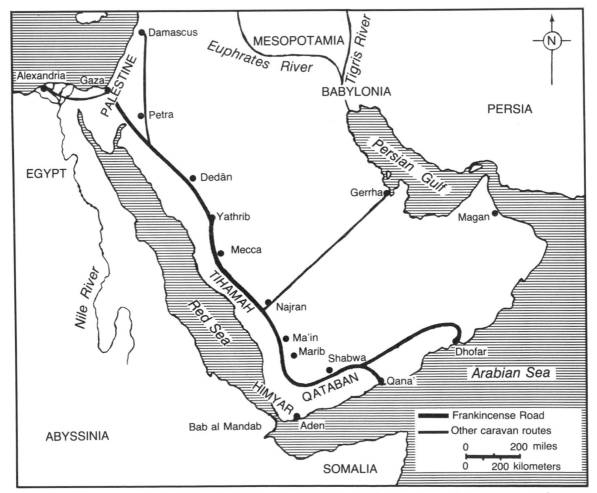

The Frankincense Road at the time of the ancient kingdoms

A caravanserai from ancient times. →

and myrrh offered to the infant Jesus by the Three Wise Men were very costly gifts. Even today, after a good meal, the Yemenite host censes each of his guests, then sprinkles them with perfume.

Able businessmen, the Yemenites of the ancient kingdoms organized the transportation of these luxury products in high demand in Egypt, Greece, Rome and Syria and elsewhere, by creating the Frankincense Road, which ran for thousands of kilometres and was followed by an unceasing traffic of caravans sometimes made up of 2,000 to 3,000 camels (or more precisely dromedaries, which have only one hump where their Asian cousins have two). Originally donkeys and mules were used, but the real desert carriers were the dromedaries, which dominated the caravan route as early as the 15th century B.C. In two months they could transport their precious, heavy loads from the Indian Ocean to the Mediterranean.

To incense and myrrh of local origin the Yemenite merchants soon added other luxury products imported from Asia via their southern ports. Navigators from Saba (as Yemen was then called) knew the secrets of the monsoon winds, and could make the return sea-voyage to India in twelve months. Articles much demanded by the rich countries of the time—silk from China, spices from India, pearls from the Arabian gulf, precious woods, gold, and the feathers of rare African birds—took to the Frankincense Road on the backs of Yemen's indefatigable dromedaries. The Yemenite merchants did not reveal the sources of these products, giving the impression that southern Arabia was overflowing with such riches. Whence the expression "Happy Arabia" or *Arabia Felix*, coined by the classical authors to designate what we today call North Yemen and South Yemen.

What organizational geniuses the Yemenites must have been to ensure the safety of caravans whose path crossed the territory of warlike tribes more or less loyal to one kingdom or another, interminable deserts where water-holes were rare, but where men and animals somehow had to stop before reaching their goal, i.e. the city of Gaza basking in the Mediterranean sun. Gaza, the Philistine city, conquered by Alexander the Great, then by Arabs in 632 A.D., by Bonaparte during his expedition to Egypt.

It is more than two thousand five hundred kilometres from the Indian Ocean to Gaza. All along the caravans' trail, from kingdom to kingdom, from one tribe to the next, defended posts had to be established, caravanserais where the camel drivers could shelter their animals and eat and rest in

A view of the old village of Marib. →

complete safety. Some of these posts became cities, among them Marib, Nagran, Mecca, Yathrib (Medina), and Petra.

Of course the post commanders levied a tax on the caravans which could be as high as 10% of the value of the merchandise they carried. In return, the caravans were protected from one post to the next. Anyone who dared to take a short-cut to avoid paying the 10 per cent risked losing his merchandise and his life as well.

The great era of the caravans ended when Greek and Roman navigators also mastered the use of the monsoons. They no longer needed the Yemenites as intermediaries, but transported the products of Asia to the Mediterranean themselves. The other great competitor of the Frankincense Road was the Silk Road. Caravans of camels (with two humps!) travelling from China or India through Persia, came to Constantinople, which had become the eastern capital of the Roman Empire. Moreover, frankincense and myrrh, Yemen's only real export products, lost their pagan-turned-Christian clientèle because the Christians used less incense in their religious ceremonies.

As often happens with civilizations, economic recession precipitated the decadence and fragmentation of the Yemenite kingdoms. The tribes regained their independence and their taste for skirmishing. The Yemenites, deprived of the riches they had earned by their trade in frankincense and myrrh (not to mention other merchandise) turned to agricultural self-suf-ficiency and the cultivation of their mountainsides.

In the 4th century A.D., Jewish and Christian missionaries alike converted some of the Himyarite kings. Early in the 6th century A.D. King Yusuf Asaar, who had embraced the Jewish faith, began to persecute the Christian Ye-menites, giving the emperor Justinian an excuse to crush his already declining kingdom: he sent in troops from a neighbouring country—Christian Ethiopia—who occupied part of Yemen for some forty years, until 570 A.D.

To defend themselves from the Ethiopians and the ascendancy of Constantinople, the Himyarites called on the Persians for help. The Persians did not need to be invited twice: after ejecting the Ethiopians they stayed on as an occupying power.

Around this time an event took place that was to have great conse-quences for Yemen, Arabia and the rest of the world: the birth of the prophet Muhammad.

CHAPTER II

SA'DA AND THE COMING OF ISLAM

*On paths none has trod, risk
your footsteps. In thoughts
none has thought, risk your
head.*

Lanza del Vasto

Jet lag has curious effects on the organism. I've been in Yemen for three days now, yet every night I wake up at three or four o'clock. I'm wide awake. I get up and read. Tonight, from my fifth-floor window, I look out at the admirable landscape of the city of Sana'a surrounded by high mountains: its proud, handsome, square houses, its fifty mosques with minarets that rise against the sky like sentinels of Allah.

At this time in the morning—and I think this is true of no other city I've seen—Sana'a is sleeping deeply, troubled by not a trace of sound. Not a rumble from a car, no bird's cry, not a drunken groan. Total silence lies over the city like a quilted robe. If a single motorcycle drove across the town from end to end, one feels it would awaken ten thousand souls in a matter of minutes...

Yet there are the dogs. Suddenly, somewhere, a flea or a tick bites a little mongrel sleeping in a ditch. He barks, and wakes a hundred others who bark in turn, waking thousands more. In a few seconds—no motorcycle could compete—the beautiful silence of Sana'a is torn to shreds by dogs. Collectively reassured by their own unholy din, the yelpers quickly tire of it and go to sleep, forgetting that it may not be so easy for a human. Again the massive silence spreads over the city. Little by little the quiet suggests sleep, and I go back to bed at dawn, the very time when the muezzins of the mosques of Sana'a climb up in the minarets to intone the call to prayer. I am not quite sure that they climb, because all the minarets have loud-speakers, and a muezzin with a single microphone could easily inundate a whole neighbourhood. It is an interminable lament that sweeps across the

The Great mosque in Sa'da. →

city like a tidal wave of sound—enough to waken all the inhabitants of Sana'a. But that's the idea: to wake people up so that they can pray to Allah, as every good Moslem should do five times a day.

To understand the history of ancient Yemen and appreciate the Yemen of today, we have, of course, to talk about Islam and the profound influence it has had on this country.

Simultaneously a religion and a political and social system, Islam arrived opportunely in Yemen. Following the period of prosperity and relative peace of the old kingdoms, Yemen found itself in utter chaos. And contributing to this general anarchy were the religious wars, provoked by the proselytism of those Yemenites who had been freshly converted to Judaism or Christianity.

Although Islam was a monotheistic religion and brought unity to the Arabs, the Moslems were divided, and after Muhammad's death the sects multiplied and throve. But these divisions were political rather than religious in nature, and the common faith brought about a certain equilibrium and unity among the warring tribes, and inspired the setting up of a great islamic caliphate in which Yemen was a part.

The prophet Muhammad began to preach the new religion to the pagans of Mecca in 610 A.D. The Semitic populations that peopled Arabia worshiped stones and statues. A black stone was considered sacred long before the coming of Islam. Today the pilgrims who come to Mecca kiss it with veneration, because, according to Moslem tradition, it was brought by the angel Gabriel to Ishmael, son of Abraham.

As one is rarely a prophet in his own country, Muhammad aroused the hostility of the ruling class of Mecca, already a goal for pilgrims who came to worship stones and statues in a temple called the Kaaba. They didn't like the competition...

In 622 A.D., Muhammad, with his disciples, fled from Mecca and took refuge in a neighbouring city, Yathrib. It was later called "the city of the prophet", which in Arabic is written Al-Medina, or Medina in English. Because of this event the year 622 became year I of the Moslem calendar. The Hijrah.

One of the many kinds of Yemenite headgear. →

Starting out from Medina, Muhammad preached the revelations of Allah throughout Arabia, and finally defeated his detractors, sometimes by force of arms, because he was also a great military leader. Eight years after he was driven out of Mecca, he returned there in triumph, the uncontested spiritual and temporal guide of the Arabian peninsula.

It was not until after the prophet's death that the revelations of Allah were compiled in a single sacred book, the Koran. The *sunna*, which contains Muhammad's teachings, is a guide for the social life of Moslems.

God in the Koran is the God of all monotheists, including Jews and Christians. He is the omnipotent Creator who was called Allah by the Arabs even before Muhammad's coming. With certain major reservations the Moslems accept the revelations of the Old and New Testaments. They believe, however, that the Koran is the last and most perfect of the divine revelations. In Islamic countries, Jews and Christians were welcome as long as they refrained from making converts. Great prophets recognized by the Moslems are: Adam, Noah, Abraham, Moses, Jesus and Muhammad. They accept many of the basic teachings of Judeo-Christianity, such as eternal life, the last judgement, heaven and hell. But they do not believe in the divinity of Jesus, who is ranked as a prophet like the others; and attribute particular authority to Abraham, one of the first prophets of monotheism and an ancestor of all Arabs through his son Ishmael, who, by the way, married a Yemenite.

A verse of the Koran sums up well the core of Islamic doctrine: "O Moslems! Believe in Allah, in his apostle, in the book He sent to him, and the Scriptures revealed before him. He who believes not in Allah, his angels, his books, his prophets and in the Last Day, is in complete error." (Koran, IV, 135.)

The Moslem religion—and perhaps this accounts for its appeal for African and Asiatic cultures—is remarkable in its great simplicity. A Moslem has five basic duties, called the "five pillars of Islam":

1. As often as possible, to profess his faith: "There is no God but God and Muhammad is his Prophet."

2. To recite his prayer five times a day, bowing his head to the ground in the direction of Mecca. The believer may pray anywhere, but preferably in a mosque.

A typical Yemenite minaret. →

42

3.   To fast for the month of Ramadan, during which it is forbidden to eat or drink between sunrise and sunset.

4.   At least once in his lifetime, to go on pilgrimage to Mecca, if capable of doing so.

5.   To give to the poor.

In addition to these five main rules, a Moslem must hold to a rigorous code of conduct which, for example, obliges him to be just and honest, and forbids adultery, usury, games of chance, drinking alcohol and eating pork.

Leader and guide of the Moslems until his death in 632 A.D., Muhammad held both temporal and spiritual power, because Islam fulfilled all society's needs. Unfortunately, the succession problem resulted in severe conflicts, which broke out twenty-five years after the prophet's death. His first successor, who adopted the title of caliph, was his father-in-law Abu Bakr, succeeded in 634 by the remarkable caliph Omar, who in turn was followed, ten years later, by Othman, assassinated in 656. The caliphs were chosen—elected, in a way of speaking—by a consultative council. This is how Muhammad's son-in-law Ali was then elected. He was the husband of Fatima, the prophet's favourite daughter. This choice was welcomed by many Moslems who believed that Ali was the natural successor to Muhammad and that the Caliphate should be hereditary. In 631, by the way, Muhammad had sent Ali to Yemen to consolidate its conversion to Islam. Because of Ali's strong personality and charisma, he soon won the hearts of the Yemenites.

As caliph, Ali had more difficulty in pacifying his rivals, among them Moawiya, governor of Syria and a relative of Othman. The two parties made war on each other, and the conflict went on so long that a schism developed. Ali's followers were called *Shiites*, who were eventually divided into several branches, among them the *Zeidis* who were particularly numerous in Yemen. The "orthodox" Moslems, i.e. those in favour of the notables electing a caliph, took the name of *Sunnites*. A branch of this group, the *Shafeis*, was inherited by Yemen. For convenience, we will use, from now on, the terms Zeidis and Shafeis.

It was Zeid, grandson of Ali and Fatima, who was behind the formation of the Zeidi sect. The conflicts that were dividing Islam favoured tribal rivalries. At times a certain number of tribes would make peace and form a kingdom, but one without fixed frontiers, which grew or diminished according to the fortunes of war.

Rammed-earth house in Sa'da. →

44

Though their recent history followed separate but parallel courses because of the imperialist aims of the Turks on the one hand and the British on the other, the two Yemens were subjected simultaneously to the powerful influence of Islam. It was a religion that had the attraction of being an Arab idea and thus familiar; which explains in part how it came to spread across Yemen like a bush-fire.

Early in the Islamic era, Yemen lived through the birth and decline of many kingdoms, all more or less dependent from one or the other of the caliphates. They often revolted against this distant religious and political domination. On the slightest provocation they showed the same will to independence which today still characterizes the Yemenites.

Kingdoms were centred around Sana'a, Sa'da, Zabid, Jiblah, Taiz and Aden. The kings built mosques and schools and even Islamic universities, some of which became renowned, like that of Zabid, to which thousands of students came from all parts to study science, mathematics, poetry and religion.

A woman distinguished herself at the head of the kingdom of Jiblah. As famous in Yemen as the Queen of Sheba, Queen Arwa reigned until 1138 A.D. when she died at the age of 92. But one of the earliest and most influencial religious leader was unquestionably Yahya al-Hadi.

A descendant of the prophet, Yahya was a Zeidi from Medina. In 897 he came to Sa'da and founded a dynasty that was to play a great role in the history of Yemen right up to the revolution of 1962. Sa'da, an old city from pre-Islamic times and a key stop along the Frankincense Road, was destined to leave its mark one day or another.

From Sana'a to Sa'da there is an excellent road (a 245 kilometre drive) running northward toward the frontier of Saudi Arabia, the land from which Islam had flooded across to Yemen like a spring torrent. We drive across high plateaus, lonely and ringed by mountains.

The first small town deserves a stop: Amran, at the junction with the road leading to Hajjah. Nibbled away by the centuries, Amran still preserves proud and majestic remains of the high mud walls which formerly surrounded it. Above the main city gate an inscription in Sabaean engraved in the stone

Young girl in Sa'da. →

46

testifies to the existence of this city in pre-Islamic times, as is the case for most of the towns on the way to Sa'da.

After Raida the road takes to the mountain and climbs bravely to a summit 2,500 metres high, then makes a quick descent to Khamir. The landscape is stony, often desert country, here and there redeemed by a green field, a miracle of irrigation. There are few cars, but we see a lone dromedary nostalgic for the old caravans with their thousands of animals prancing along the desert trails; and here is a little shepherdess all dressed in black chasing her white goats. A gentle, innocent scene, evoking the pastoral poetry which Yahya al-Hadi must have loved, as did most of the imams that followed him. An imam was supposed to be a holy man, though some were bloody tyrants. Several of them had a weakness for poetry and even wrote it themselves.

From one village to the next the architecture of the houses changes and grows hospitable. The mini-skyscrapers in hewn stone give way to more modest mud constructions, with only the foundations or first storeys in stone. Instead of the large and numerous windows found in Sana'a and its environs, here we find more conventional openings, sometimes small and round like spectacles, sometimes narrow and vertical, like the arrow slits from which, in the heroic days, one could shoot at assailants from a neighbouring tribe.

We drive through Huth, from which a dirt road leaves for the Shahara mountains, the highest of which reaches 3,000 metres. This excursion calls for a cross-country vehicle, but a sporty traveller would do well to make it on foot starting from the village of Al Qabai. It's a five-hour climb to the top, but it's worth the effort, if only to admire the incredible stone bridge built in the 17th century, literally joining two mountains.

We arrive at Sa'da around noon. The sun is at its zenith, the heat is intense, and the streets are almost deserted at this hour when people are eating or resting in the cool of their thick-walled houses.

In the pre-Islamic age, Sa'da was already an important stop on the old Frankincense Road. When the Imam Yahya al-Hadi made it the capital of his kingdom and the religious centre of the Zeidis, he hastened to surround it with an earthen wall that was to protect if for a century. There remains

Typical house in Sa'da. →

48

an interesting segment of it from which one gets an astonishing view of the city. Even today students come as visitors to the beautiful al-Haldi mosque to study Zeidism.

One simply must go and idle among the stalls of the market, to admire— or buy for a song—marvellous old silver jewelry, observe the women haggling and sometimes paying with Maria-Teresa *Thalers*. Introduced to Yemen by the Turks during the Ottoman occupation, these Austrian coins are still circulating, and are also used to make heavy, intricate necklaces. But since the revolution of 1962 the *Thalers* are growing rare, replaced by the Yemenite riyal.

Outside the walls, one must not forget a Moslem cemetery unusual because of its tombstones decorated with arabesques, and the impressive dome tombs that watch over the eternal sleep of pious *ulemas* or members of the royal family. As for the remains of Yahya al-Hadi, they are buried at the centre of the Great Mosque.

The real enchantment of Sa'da is in walking in the old neighbourhoods with their narrow, silent streets, and no cars in sight. Admirable earth houses, rarely more than two or three storeys high. Some earthen walls are scored with parallel, undulating lines, and pierced with small windows. The biggest windows have the honour of being enclosed by a *shubbak*, a handsome bay of wooden fretwork. Whitened with plaster, the merlons of the parapets shine like snow.

From the streets one enters alleys so narrow that one could almost shake hands from a window on one side to that on the other. Underfoot is sand and one walks silently, as in a dream. There are few foreigners in Sa'da, and during our visit we saw none. Yet our presence seems not to bother or astonish anyone. The men greet us gravely and respond graciously if we risk saying *"assalamou alaikom"* ("peace be with you"). The children, for their part, approach us uninhibited, and follow us in giggling groups for two or three blocks, trying out the bits of English they have learned in school: "What is your name? Where do you come from? How do you do?" They are often very good-looking, and the little girls especially are charming with their hoods that make them look like miniature monks.

On our way back, a stop in a tiny village, built entirely of earth and dominated by the round towers I first took for silos for grain or forage. They

Details of the Ashraffiya mosque. →

are living quarters. One of them, two storeys high looks like a carnival figure with a protuberant nose and two tiny, round windows like sparkling, malicious eyes. I don't know if this old tower ever evoked the carnival in the minds of other travellers: everyone sees creatures and things in a unique way. But as long as I live, that enormous, grotesque head will reappear in my mind's eye, and no one will know why I'm grinning to myself...

CHAPTER III

HAJJAH AND THE REIGN OF THE IMAMS

*Men's natures are similar; it is
their customs that divide them.*

Confucius

Hajjah is a good place for approaching the Yemen of the imams, who found in this town and in the neighbouring tribes the surest allies of their regime.

Each tribe was a little state with its own laws and customs, its economic and political autonomy, its peasant-warriors, and its leader, the *sheik*. Conciliator and arbiter, at the same time judge and military chief, the *sheik* is elected by the ruling class of the tribe and must take into account the desires of his electors. If he does not, he risks being deprived of his powers and, in exceptional cases, assassinated.

In Yemen, the imam was above all a spiritual leader, and in order to acquire temporal power over a certain number of tribes and weld them into a kingdom, he had to be accepted by the *sheiks*—or vanquish them on the battlefield! What was more, the chiefs of the vassal tribes considered the imam as the head of a "federal" government with limited powers, and insisted on participating in the election of his successor. Only a few very strong imams managed to found true dynasties by imposing a "crown prince" on their subjects contrary to tradition.

Our driver today, a young man, is called Muhammad, and he has brought along a boy of his own age, Faisal, who knows a little English. Efficient, smiling, polite, thin as a rake, Muhammad wears a long, white robe that floats on his skinny body and makes him look like a puppet.

From Sana'a we take the road to the north, toward Sa'da, as far as Amran, where there is a great Moslem feast. Families in their Sunday best

A view of Hajjah. →

53

are coming back from the mosque. They linger in the square, and greet and embrace other families in their finest togs. The fathers are in a generous mood and buy lollipops for their children. Others go to the cemetery to meditate at the grave of a loved one. How can they find their way in this enormous field entirely covered with anonymous stones?

On leaving Amran we head straight west, toward the Red Sea. The road is still paved, but it now starts zig-zagging along the slopes of high mountains like a snake gone mad. It was quarried directly in the rock, which means that we are driving constantly between a wall of solid rock, from which enormous blocks sometimes crash on the road, and a precipice several hundred metres deep. There is no lack of strong emotions, especially when Muhammad decides to peel a banana while passing a tank truck on a hairpin curve!

But never in my long lifetime of travelling have I seen mountain scenery of such gripping beauty. I have crossed the Andes twenty times, "my" Rockies hold no more secrets for me, I have seen the Sierra Madre, the Atlas range, the Alps, Kilimanjaro, the Himalayas, but nothing has so impressed me as the landscapes between Amran and Hajjah, especially the stretch from Kohlan, a village perched 2,400 metres high, to the valley of the wadi Sherec which is 1,000 metres above sea level. The great rocks around us change colour with the altitude. Sometimes black with glints of violet, they turn to greens, reds, ochres and grays.

We stop for a long pause at the summit of a mountain from which we see the road descend in serpentine curves to the floor of the valley one or two thousand metres below. And it was not just to please Muhammad that I exclaimed, "Muhammad, believe me, I have never in the world seen anything so beautiful!"

Hajjah is a unique city, very impressive with its enormous citadel built in the very centre, on the highest hill. It was here, in 1948, that the Imam Ahmad had assembled the warriors of the nearby tribes to save his throne and march to punish Sana'a, where his father, imam Yahya Hamid al-Din had just been assassinated. How many political prisoners had rotted for an eternity in the subterranean cells of the citadel? How many died in the most inhuman conditions? How many hostages were held there for years? The imams had perfected an efficient system to ensure the loyalty of the *sheiks*: as hostages, they took their eldest sons...

A peasant of Attur. →

56

Belonging to an old dynasty of more than a hundred imams, Yahya and Ahmed were the last who actually reigned and played a major role in Yemen's history. We have seen how the first Zeidi imam, Yahya al-Hadi, had established a kingdom at the end of the 9th century, with its capital in Sa'da some 270 kilometres from here. A very courageous man, erudite and pious, al-Hadi was a direct descendant of Ali and Fatima. Like all the imams that succeeded him up to 1962, he belonged to the Zeidi branch of Islam. The members of the royal family were, of course, Zeidis, as were the big landowners and high officials.

Thanks to his strong personality, the Imam al-Hadi succeeded in rallying a large number of warlike tribes to his cause. In 900 and 909 A.D. he tried in vain to conquer Sana'a. In 911 he died in Sa'da without having expanded his kingdom as much as he would have liked.

It is worth noticing that Yemen survived occupation or attempted occupation by all the great imperialist powers of successive epochs. In 24 B.C. Yemen and particularly Saba were the goals of an unsuccessful expedition by the Roman emperor Augustus. In 1507 A.D. the Portuguese occupied a small port on the south shore of Yemen, but did not succeed in taking Aden, an ideal position for controlling the trade between India and the countries of the Mediterranean. After the Portuguese came the Egyptians. In 1517 the Mamelukes came to Yemen, only to be replaced by the Turks of the Ottoman empire, who were more successful: in 1538 their fleet attacked Aden while their armies captured Tihama, Taiz and even Sana'a.

This first Turkish occupation was to last a century, but thanks to the leadership of the imams, the tribes rose against their occupier and the Imam's kingdom finally expanded to include all of Yemen, from Najran to Hadhramaut, as the Himyarite kingdom had done a thousand years earlier.

By 1598 Qasim, a remarkable imam, had succeeded in liberating a dozen provinces but the Turks were persistent and continued to harry the Imam's armies. Less well-equipped, the Yemenites were none the less good fighters. Finally the Turks resigned themselves to signing a ten-year truce with the Imam, during which he reigned over a large part of the country. That was in 1608, the same year in which Champlain came to found Québec in the name of the King of France.

Facade of a palace of the Imam. →

The Imam Muhammad, Qasim's successor, took up the war against the Turks until their departure from Yemen in 1635. They might never have come back if the British had not captured the port of Aden in 1839. The Ottoman Empire was influential on both shores of the Red Sea, and felt itself threatened by the presence of a great power in this strategic area. The second Turkish occupation began in 1848. The rivalry between the two imperialist powers is directly responsible for the creation of an artificial frontier between two parts of Yemen which later became North Yemen and South Yemen.

On the other hand, it was the threat from abroad, whether from Egypt, Turkey or elsewhere, which finally led to rallying-around an imam by the Yemenites. Chosen in 1890, the Imam al-Mansur declared a holy war against the Turks, who were Moslems but not Arabs. Perhaps without realizing it, he thus contributed to the flowering of the Yemenite nationalism that was to give birth to modern—and republican!—Yemen.

Then came the Imam Yahya, son of al-Mansur, a man who was out of the ordinary, a tough warrior and an authoritarian and pitiless head of state. His reign, which lasted more than forty years, helped to build the Yemen of today. As he lived in the first half of our century, one might imagine that his country was at last about to emerge from its dark ages, and join the developments of modern times, including becoming industrialized. But Yahya had other priorities...

Let's try for a moment to imagine what Yemen was like in 1904, practically closed to foreigners, except the Turks, who had battered down the gates and maintained their presence by the force of arms.

First, it was hard to get around in this mountainous country. Roads were few and rough. Not until 1923 did Imam Yahya allow the importation of a few motor vehicles, over which he kept strict control, for security reasons as well as to make a profit from transporting travellers and goods. He had forbidden the construction of a railway—even today Yemen has none. An elementary telegraph system linked the main cities, but the Imam had the most serious reservations about the use of radio.

Medical care was virtually nonexistent. Yahya authorized the construction of a small hospital in Hodeida in 1912, then one in Sana'a and in Taiz. The doctors came from Europe and the hospitals mainly served the

Whitewashed with plaster, the cornices gleam like diadems. →

rich. There were hardly any schools. In the mosques, the *ulemas* taught children Arabic writing and the Koran. Veiled, hidden and illiterate, the women's duty was to bring children into the world, look after household chores and work in the fields. Wells and cisterns were far from the houses, and the simple job of supplying the family with water was an onerous daily task.

The Yemenites were good farmers and managed with more or less success to feed themselves, but suffered from certain dietary deficiencies. They were continually under pressure from the tax collectors who saw to the financing of the Imam's needs and those of the Sana'a government, which, by the way, did not have a national budget. There was no banking system, and all transactions were in cash, i.e. the silver *Thalers* bearing the profile of Maria Teresa of Austria and dated 1780.

A religious and political leader at the same time, Imam Yahya was under a strict obligation to govern according to the Koran. In practice, he interpreted Koranic law in his own way, and often behaved like a despot. He played one tribe against another and his reign was one of corruption, patronage and fear. Those who had the audacity to dispute his authority or his legitimacy did not live long: their heads were cut off and exposed in public. The prisons were packed with mere suspects who lived in atrocious conditions until they died of untreated ailments, prolonged undernourishment or the results of torture. In Sana'a the Imam held thousands of hostages, sons of tribal chiefs, provincial governors or members of his own family. On the slightest hostile move by the father his son was tortured and beheaded.

No doubt these methods enabled Yahya to stay in power for a long time, but this was also because he had built up an army and fought vigorously against the Turkish occupation. At the very beginning of his reign he besieged Sana'a and forced the Turks to surrender in 1905. The Ottoman army re-captured the city a few months later, but Yahya persistently harassed the Turkish troops until the two parties, in 1911, signed a treaty which was to last ten years. But in 1918, the Turks, big losers in the first world war, left Yemen for good, allowing it to become the first independent Arab state.

An odd sidelight: the Imam kept by him in Sana'a some hundreds of Turkish advisers... including the last governor! Later, in order to modernize the Yemenite army, he called in military advisers from Iraq and Syria. These were sensible moves, since Yahya, though a good soldier, was not competent

Terrace agriculture near Hajjah. →

62

to reorganize his kingdom on any kind of "modern" basis. He went so far as to appoint a cabinet of ministers, but entrusted them with only limited responsibilities.

The end of the second Turkish occupation could not wipe out the recollection that the British had moved into Aden in 1839, which incidentally provoked the return of the Turks. Originally attached to the Indian government, this symbol of British imperialism became a Crown colony in 1937. Gradually, Aden extended its influence on the southern tribes, which became British protectorates.

Perhaps weary of making war on all sides, the Imam finally made peace with his Northern and Southern neighbours and reestablished security and peace in his kingdom. Yahya knew his people well, and realized that to keep them under his rule and ensure its future he had to protect Yemen from any ideas that had infiltrated from the outer world. Opened just a crack by the Turkish occupation, the country snapped shut like an oyster.

Despite his determination to keep the people of Yemen in ignorance of what was going on in the rest of the world, Yahya could not dispense with the services of his advisers from other Arab countries or (to a lesser degree) from European countries, nor could he prevent a small number of young Yemenites from studying abroad or from spending time there as migrant workers. He was even so imprudent as to send young Yemenite officers to the Baghdad military college. One of these, Abdullah al-Sallal, became a leader of the revolution of 1962... These small fissures allowed revolutionary ideas to filter slowly into the medieval fortress that was Imam Yahya's Yemen.

Paradoxically, he was anxious to obtain recognition on an international scale. He actually allowed a small number of diplomats and foreign businessmen access to Sana'a, and permitted Yemen to become a member, in 1945, of the Arab League and, in 1947, of the United Nations.

These overtures, timid as they were, went against the grain of Yahya, but this intelligent man, sly and better informed than one might expect, had understood that a breeze of reform coming from abroad could, sooner or later, threaten his régime and his dynasty. He was aware of the activities of the Movement of Free Yemenites, founded in Aden in 1944, which included Yemenites from North and South, traditionalist and progressive Moslem

Egg vendor in a market. →

elements, military and religious, intellectual and working-class leaders, and Zeidis and Shafeis. These reformers demanded the democratization of the two Yemens, but they would have accepted a constitutional monarchy—a notion that must have given the shudders to Imam Yahya!

Already in his eighties and in ill health, he wanted to avoid succession problems by choosing his heir: Ahmad, the most detested but the most resolute of his sons. This decision infringed upon the most ancient traditions of the Zeidi imamate and provoked opposition on the part of the people and—even more—among the nobles. A new imam must without fail be elected by the *ulemas* and other notables who were descendants of the prophet Muhammad by the branch of Ali and Fatima. The candidate chosen is the one who best fulfils the fourteen conditions laid down by the Zeidi tradition. For example, to become an imam one must be: male, freeborn, healthy in mind and body, just, pious, generous and scholarly, a taxpayer, an excellent warrior, a competent jurist, a good administrator, and, to be sure, a descendant of the family of Ali. Nowadays in democratic and other regimes, less is required to become a head of state...

It goes without saying that Yahya had trouble demonstrating that his son Ahmad lived up to even half of these conditions, especially as others among his sons and the notables of the time seemed to come closer to ressembling the ideal candidate. But he refused good advice and proclaimed Ahmad "crown prince".

A year later, in 1948, Yahya was shot by assassins and, in the absence of Ahmad, who was in Taiz, a "usurper" tried to take power with the help of the *ulemas* and the Free Yemenites. The crown prince, who was in Taiz, of which he was the governor, gathered together a few soldiers and marched to Hajjah, where he recruited the formidable warriors of the Hashid and Bakil tribes, loyal partisans of the Zeidi imams. He dashed on to Sana'a and, later, allowed his warriors to behead his rival and all who might be his accomplices, and to pillage and sack the city while, prudently, he returned to Taiz, which he made his capital.

After this hasty review of the Yemen of the imams, we find ourselves, appropriately, in Hajjah, at the foot of this citadel which symbolizes the power of the long Zeidi dynasty as it nears its end.

Two dromedaries on the Barakish trail. →

All around the citadel stand handsome, ancient houses four or five storeys high, still inhabited, and round stone towers that one doesn't find in the Sana'a region.

Let's have lunch in a brand-new hotel built on the summit of another hill, where we have a breathtaking view. From somewhere in the city below comes the sound of a happy crowd, punctuated by the occasional gunshot. Faisal smiles: "It's a holiday, the men are having a little fun." In many parts of Yemen the men still wear, in addition to their impressive *jambia*, rifles carried by a shoulder-strap. They only use them now for shooting in the air on feast days, but no more than forty years ago they were in action saving the Imam Ahmad, and in the sixties these veteran warriors fought for seven years: partisans of the imamate against partisans of the republic.

We start back on the road to Sana'a, which has quite an altered appearance, no doubt because the light has changed... and the precipices are now on the other side! Muhammad often has to jam on the brakes to avoid ploughing into a herd of goats or sheep or dromedaries.

With no warning, Muhammad leaves the highway and stops in a small village. He and Faisal give me to understand that they want to buy their supply of *qat* to end the day on a tranquil note. I go with them into a dark shop where I observe an intricate process of bargaining. Muhammad picks up a bouquet of *qat*, examines it on all sides, sniffs at the roots, and slowly caresses the leaves with his fingers. Without understanding a word I can see that Muhammad is putting on the airs of an expert and trying to run down the merchandise to get it at a bargain price. After fifteen minutes haggling he gives up and we leave the shop empty-handed.

We stop again at a roadside shanty surrounded by rubbish. Muhammad and Faisal bargain again without success. Failing *qat* we settle for orange soda-pop. Taking some care where I step, I make my way around behind the shanty to admire yet another extraordinary view. There is a kind of annex, and I peek inside. To my great surprise I realize that it is a modest *mafraj* built of concrete blocks: a living-room with cushions along the walls on which one reclines to chew *qat*. As in the more sumptuous *mafrajs* that I've visited, immense windows look out on a landscape that even the rich in Sana'a cannot buy. In a corner there are three or four hookahs and an amphora filled with water which the vessel keeps cool. This afternoon the

A village to the west of Hajjah. →

shopkeeper will be there with a dozen or so friends, they will chew *qat*, smoke a pipe or two and chat happily for hours and hours.

On first sight, such daily relaxation sessions seem inappropriate for these former warriors, rough peasants who wring a living out of the mountain soil, these brave men who do not hesitate to leave their country for a year or two in order to labour hard in some foreign land where they are the most welcome of guest workers—not to mention the refined intellectuals of Sana'a or the acute businessmen of Hodeida or elsewhere. Yet no doubt they are right to take time for a good discussion or a good laugh—in short, time to live!

CHAPTER IV

TAIZ AND THE REVOLUTION

A kingdom can have but one crown; I will uncrown my rival or he will uncrown me.

Pope Innocent III

Accompanied by a high official and by our driver (and friend) Abdullah, we go to see Taiz, the second-largest city in Yemen and the one that the Imam Ahmad preferred to Sana'a. Four hours of good paved road (260 kilometres), much of it in high mountains, plunging me once more into the horrors many times experienced in the Andes, Colombia, Ecuador and Bolivia: hairpin roads skirting precipices several hundred metres deep, and terrifyingly dangerous traffic due to the daredevil style of Yemenite drivers (and those of the Third World in general). All our Yemenite friends agree: Abdullah is one of the best drivers in the country. Before the revolution he was the favourite driver of the Imam Ahmad. No doubt because of his excellent reputation he went directly from serving the monarchy to serving the republic. A sort of Talleyrand of the internal combustion era! Be that as it may, Abdullah feels that no vehicle should be faster than ours. He passes two trucks in succession in a 45° curve. Rarely, but sometimes, he passes on the *right*. He speeds up in the villages, especially if the streets are crowded, and clears the road with furious blasts of his horn.

The road to Taiz is worth a few risks. A landscape of wild, unspoiled beauty, bathed in light. Some mountains are prodigious sculptures: for hundreds, even thousands of years, peasants have terraced entire slopes, making farming possible in this arid, mountainous countryside, and giving the landscape a strange relief, like the altitude lines on a topographical map.

Having crossed the first mountain range, we drive over a plateau with only sparse vegetation in this season. Nothing but stones, sand and dust. Only the bright blue of the sky prevents us from despairing of this inhospitable

The Ashraffiya mosque in Taiz. →

71

land. "When it rains, all this turns green," Hassan, our travelling-companion, assures us, "and the April monsoons are coming."

In the course of the day we would actually see three or four tractors in the fields ("Volvos donated by Sweden"), but cultivation is also done as in Biblical times, with a small plough drawn by two donkeys. By way of contrast, the brand-new roofs of large, modern hen-houses shine in the sunlight.

We stop for a few minutes in a village where Hassan makes a phone call, perhaps to settle the details of our brief visit to Taiz. While we wait, Abdullah brings us cups of boiling-hot, very sweet tea which we enjoy while admiring the architectural harmony of this humble village. The block-like houses of four or five storeys are often built encircling the summit of a hill so that they almost form a wall, a sort of ingenious fortress easy to defend against attacks by the warrior tribes of former times. Almost always built of stone quarried from the mountain itself, they seem to be extensions of it, hewn from the very rock. Unlike the usual dwellings found in Arab countries, those of the Yemenites have windows looking out on all sides, so as to hide nothing of the austere countryside they love so dearly.

Hassan turns out to be an excellent guide. His job keeps him well-informed on political matters, but he is a poet as well. At university he studied French, English and Arabic literature. Like all officials here, he works from 8:00 a.m. to 2:00 p.m. "In the afternoon I pursue other interests. I edit a literary magazine, I write and publish poems." There is nothing astonishing about this in a country where poetry, especially popular poetry, has always been important. To celebrate a wedding or the visit of a high official the village poet comes to recite his poems, often written for the occasion. It even happens that an official petition is submitted in poetic form. It is said that a group of Yemenite intellectuals, no doubt republicans, had been imprisoned by the Imam Ahmad after the assassination of his father Yahya. They languished in the prison-fortress of Hajjah with little hope of coming out alive. The Imam remained untouched by their appeals for clemency until the day when they sent him a supplication in verse. This Nero loved poetry!

The Yemenites are also music lovers. Theirs is quite different from the rest of Arab music. In the villages it is not unusual to see a poet being accompanied by a little group of local musicians. These traits of the Yemenite

Turbans in Taiz. →

character would seem to be in contradiction with the ferocious air still cultivated by these former warriors. But in fact they are a gentle, peaceful people. Crime is rare; and how many countries remain on earth where, as in Yemen, a foreigner can stroll without risk in any city at any hour of the day or night? The hospitality of Yemenites toward foreigners, their kindness, their generosity, are qualities that place this country in a category apart.

I mentioned the perils of driving, but the fact remains that the road was well-paved, and built some fifteen years ago by the Federal Republic of Germany. Until the fifties there were practically no roads fit to drive on in Yemen. Today the main cities are linked by a modern network of highways.

Vegetation is still rare, though there is more of it as we approach Taiz. Here and there, amid the vast, arid, rocky spaces, we see a miracle in the form of a corn or sorghum field, or a garden of glistening lettuce. A few languid dromedaries remind us of the desert's proximity. From time to time, on a strategic hill, the ruins of a Turkish fortress. The Ottoman empire had stretched its tentacles to here.

What makes Yemen different from the rest of desert Arabia are the high mountains that form its backbone. The highest peak, Nabi Shaib near Sana'a, is 4,000 metres high. This geographical irregularity in a mostly flat peninsula gave Yemen its agricultural vocation and played a considerable role in protecting its tribes against invaders.

The country has a pleasant climate: dry in winter (November to February), it receives a good deal of rain in April and August, which makes it possible to cultivate the valleys, the high plateaus, and even the terraced mountain-sides. But agriculture would have been much more difficult if, since time immemorial, the Yemenites had not learned how to conserve rain water and distribute it intelligently. Terrace farming has the double advantage of retaining the runoff and preventing erosion.

It is very wrong of us to rush along this historic route without making more stops in the small towns, which from a distance are all alike, but on closer acquaintance are chock-full of their own history and architectural marvels. A hundred kilometres from Sana'a we discover Dhamar, which dates back to pre-Islamic days, and at times was the capital of the Zeidi imams.

A minaret de Taiz. →

A little farther on, the city of Dhafar, capital of the ancient kingdom of the Himyarites, which from 115 B.C. to 525 A.D. dominated a large part of Yemen; and the town of Ibb, capital of the province of the same name, built on a hill from which the view is stunning; and Jiblah, where the great Queen Arwa reigned in the 11th century.

After crossing another mountain by way of a pass at an altitude of 2,000 metres, we descend toward the marvellous Taiz, situated at 1,400 metres. The dynasty of the Rasulids (1229-1454) had its capital here. It was also the choice of the Imam Ahmad (1948-1962), whose death coincided with the tardy end of the feudal age and the entry of Yemen into the modern era.

As we approach Taiz we should say something about Imam Ahmad and the events that marked his reign and determined the future of all Yemen.

On the death of his father the Imam Yahya, Ahmad was the governor of Taiz. Yahya, contrary to tradition, had also named him "crown prince", which the ulemas did not really accept. As soon as the death of Yahya was confirmed they hastened to proclaim Abdullah al-Wazir as Imam, which pleased the Free Yemenites who were refugees in Aden. Convinced that the new Imam was going to liberalize the régime, they made haste to get to Sana'a.

Because of his brutality Ahmad was the most detested of Imam Yahya's sons. Yahya himself reproached him for his cruelty and exhorted him to mend his ways. Why did Yahya appoint him as heir when he had other sons whose tyrannical instincts were less obvious? Probably he knew that to survive as imam it was necessary to have Ahmad's implacable character.

Ahmad made quick work of crushing the man who had been his rival for only a few days. He beheaded a few dozen opponents, had himself proclaimed Imam in Sana'a, let his warriors sack the city and left for Taiz where he set up his capital, 160 kilometres from Aden but 260 from his last massacre.

Ahmad's reign strangely resembled that of his father Yahya. The new Imam had the same mistrust of foreign influences, and, without succeeding completely, he slowed down all attempts at liberalization and development

A spice market in Taiz. →

78

in Yemen. He used the time-tested methods of his predecessors: the hostage system, corruption, imprisonment of suspects and decapitation of "traitors."

Ahmad's relations with his British "neighbours" in Aden had their ups and downs. He bitterly reproached the Aden authorities for their support of the Free Yemenites, avowed enemies of his régime. By way of reprisal he gave his support to the tribes of the South, which, though they came under the Aden protectorate, skirmished against the British. For Ahmad this was also a way of reminding the latter that they were occupying a part of his kingdom, as South Yemen had been under the control of the imamate for a hundred years.

But the British had been in Aden for over a century. Aden's strategic value had always been obvious to these builders of empire—the one on which the sun never set. The British were not much interested in the fate of the little kingdoms and back-country tribes, which they were content to reduce to vassals to protect Aden.

In 1954, in a final effort to extend its influence in the region and keep control of Aden, London tried to unite these small states in a broad federation, which would then become a dominion with democratic structures but having at its head a British governor who would have the less pretentious title of High Commissioner. Too late: the fever of independence had already reached the warrior tribes!

It goes without saying that the Imam Ahmad was categorically opposed to this scheme which ignored his plans and would sooner or later be a threat to his autocratic régime. With the support of Egypt and the Arab League, Ahmad put pressure on the chiefs of the tribes in the South not to join this federation imposed on the country by a despised colonial power, and he continued to harass it in the frontier regions.

In reality Imam Ahmad and his predecessors cared little about national unity, a concept that had no meaning for a group of tribes fiercely attached to their autonomy and their own identity. The imams' prime concern was for their personal power and the search for ways to expand it in all directions.

After the deposition of King Farouk in 1952, and especially when Nasser became head of the new Egyptian republic, Ahmad realized that his enemies had found a powerful ally in Egypt. The Free Yemenites were

Two noble peasants. →

already broadcasting from Aden, and now came Radio Cairo encouraging the revolutionary inclinations of Yemen. Ahmad at once ordered all radios in public places confiscated...

In 1955 he narrowly survived a coup d'état organized by his half-brother Abdullah. Imam Ahmad's son, al-Badr, then governor of Hodeida, sped to Hajjah, the heart of the old reservoir of warriors loyal to the Zeidi imams, and raised an army to defend his father. Following this event, Ahmad, indifferent to tradition as his father had been, proclaimed al-Badr "crown prince".

Al-Badr played a key role in the life of the kingdom. In 1956 he established contact with the USSR, which hastened to send arms to the Imam, allowing him to carry on his small war against the British more efficiently. Thanks to the prince's influence, increasing numbers of Soviet, Chinese and Egyptian experts arrived in Yemen. The Imam continued to mistrust these guests who were not known to be great admirers of the monarchical system, but these modest openings on the outside world increased the credit of the crown prince with the reformers and even with the republicans who were active in Aden and Cairo.

The Egyptians modernized Yemen's army—no doubt in the process infecting it with a few revolutionary ideas!—while the Chinese patiently built a new mountain road between Sana'a and Hodeida. When the construction was finished, Imam Ahmad promptly quarreled with the countries who had contributed to the modernization of Yemen: Ahmad refused to pay the bill, and sent the foreign technicians home with their fine ideologies.

In 1958, to the astonishment of all, Yemen joined the United Arab States, an ephemeral federation created by Nasser which already included Egypt and Syria. Ahmad never took this move of his seriously, but it brought him certain immediate political advantages by neutralizing Egypt and other Arab countries that were against his totalitarian and retrogressive régime. He was a master of the art of taking without giving anything in return, flirting with the socialist countries while establishing diplomatic relations with the United States.

In 1959 Imam Ahmad made an urgent visit to Rome to receive medical treatment. He was suffering from arthritis, but had also become addicted to morphine while using it as a pain-killer.

A mosque in Taiz. →

Appointed regent in his father's absence, prince al-Badr intensified his program for developing the country, with the help of the Egyptians and with Nasser's blessing. This unexpected action caused great discontent among the royalist elites. They brought up the question of his "crown prince" status, imposed by Ahmad, mentioning the names of other notables who could, one day, succeed the Imam. There were revolts in Hodeida and Taiz, but al-Badr had not the necessary authority to repress them.

When Ahmad returned from Rome he put down the revolts with his usual brutality, causing a few heads to roll and reasserting his power over the kingdom. For a time al-Badr had to retire to his tent, but did not lose his title as crown prince. No one else in the royal family found favour in the eyes of the Imam.

Ahmad's health continued to deteriorate, some tribes renewed their revolt, the subversive influence of the Egyptians and the Free Yemenites made itself increasingly felt, certain young army officers dreamed of conspiracy, and in the world's eyes the imamate personified tyranny and corruption. In short, medieval Yemen was on the point of shaking off the yoke of its terrible imam.

In 1961 Ahmad was obliged to consult his doctors—all foreigners—in the small hospital of Hodeida. A handful of conspirators were waiting for him there and opened fire. The Imam fell, hit by five bullets. Endowed with astonishing stamina, the old man survived. Those who had been in on the plot had less luck: they were beheaded or committed suicide.

In that same year, still unconvinced by Nasser's "socialism" and "modernism", Ahmad burned his bridges with Egypt. He suspected that the attention paid to him and his son al-Badr by Egypt had little to do with strengthening Yemen's monarchy. Ahmad was right: at the first opportunity Egypt was to lend its support, not to a casual reformer like al-Badr, but to a more authentic revolutionary of humble background: Abdullah al-Sallal.

On September 20, 1962, the Voice of Arabs informed the world that the Imam Ahmad had died of natural causes and that he was succeeded by the crown prince al-Badr. The latter at once announced a number of reforms intended to make people forget his father's tyranny. Taken by surprise, Nasser sent a message of congratulation to the new imam, but his revolutionary propaganda against Yemen continued loud and strong.

A proud inhabitant of Shibam. →

The reign of the Imam al-Badr, the last Zeidi imam, was a short one. Barely a week after Ahmad's death, his own army attacked his palace in Sana'a with tanks which demolished the two top floors of the building. Al-Badr, however, succeeded in escaping disguised as a soldier. The revolutionaries thought he had been crushed by the rubble, and were for a time unwilling to admit that he was still alive. But he was, and this upset the plans of the leader of the revolution, Abdullah al-Sallal, a senior officer who had pursued his military studies in Iraq, where he had, no doubt, acquired his republican convictions.

On September 26, 1962, North Yemen took the name of the Yemen Arab Republic, and a few days later the new régime formed a government that was quickly recognized by several Arab countries, the socialist countries and, finally, by the United States.

In November 1962, however, the world was forced to admit that the Imam al-Badr was very much alive. He was organizing the tribes that had remained loyal, in part because the Imam represented the legitimate spiritual authority. Thanks to support from King Faisal of Saudi Arabia, al-Badr succeeded in getting control of the main cities north of Sana'a and the cities of Marib and Harib in the eastern part of the country.

The republicans, for their part, with the help of eventually 40,000 Egyptian soldiers, controlled the central part of the country, the coast of the Red Sea, and the three largest cities: Hodeida, Sana'a and Taiz.

Because the Imam al-Badr did not die in Sana'a as planned, a long and bloody civil war was inflicted on Yemen for the next seven years. It had disastrous effects on an economy that was mainly agricultural. The production of the famous mokha coffee dropped dramatically.

Finally, after a treaty between Egypt and Saudi Arabia, the Egyptian troops left Yemen on December 7, 1967. The monarchy had lost, the Yemen Arab Republic had won.

At about the same time the British left Aden, and the federation of small states they had tried to form became a republic with Marxist leanings, which took the name of the People's Democratic Republic of Yemen. Since then the two Yemens have been trying to find a way to unite in a single state these two parts of one and the same country.

A jambia shop. →

Last capital of the imams, the radiant city of Taiz (178,000 inhabitants) sprawls around the foot of Mount Sabir, which rises to a height of 3,200 metres. The city's tall houses are built of stone hewn from gray volcanic rock, embellished with another variety as white as milk. From the top of a hill we admire it in silence for a long moment, until our host arrives, a member of parliament who has been informed of my brief stop in his city. He is also an engineer, manager of the highways department in the region. He has had an excellent lunch prepared for us in a bungalow reserved for special guests. Then, in his car, we climb almost to the summit of Mount Sabir, where the view of Taiz and the mountain ranges surrounding it is of an indescribable beauty. The viewer looks in silence, contemplating, admiring, trembling, wondering if it is real or if it might not be a Cecil B. de Mille set for some prodigious Biblical fantasy, or a dream city by Dali where a hundred minarets point their ancient fingers at the sky amid the domed mosques, white and round as giant meringues.

We tour the old town which is surrounded by a wall with seven gates. Until the revolution of 1962, they were locked every night at sundown and opened again at dawn. An admirable architectural ensemble, dominated by the Al-Qahira citadel. Before a very beautiful old four-storey house, still inhabited, I ask how old it might be. "Seven hundred years, maybe more," replies our friend the member of parliament.

It is already three o'clock and we would like to be in Sana'a before nightfall. "But your can't leave Taiz without chewing a little *qat*! And seeing my *mafraj*..."

It just happens to be *qat* time. All over Yemen the same thing is happening: a group of men as diverse as one can imagine are sitting around on cushions and following a kind of ritual. Who are the people in this hall of guests?

A Yemenite engineer and member of parliament, 48.

A Montréal businessman, 43.

A Yemenite official and occasional poet, 28.

A Mercedes driver, stated age between 50 and 53.

The fortress of Sumara between Sana'a and Taiz. →

88

A Canadian senator, 63 but doesn't believe it.

And a few unidentified guests.

As if by enchantment bouquets of *qat* fall in front of each of us. I am quite aware that *qat* is a very soft drug, reputed to be a medicinal plant and praised by the Yemenites for its therapeutic virtues and its euphoric effects. I know, but I have a horror of all drugs (except perhaps Cutty Sark with water!), and I hesitate a moment before chewing the spray of small leaves my host holds out to me. They explain to me the many virtues of *qat*: "It's a stimulant for warriors..." Yes, but I'm a pacifist! "It's an excellent cure for melancholy..." Melancholy? Never heard of it. "It's an intellectual stimulant..." Oh well, in that case...

The Yemenites have already chewed several dozen leaves into a wad which one holds between cheek and gums for hours on end. I do my best, but I swallow more of the bitter leaves than I manage to keep. Within arm's reach is a bottle of mineral water, indispensable while chewing this astringent plant. In front of each place is a *qat* spitoon shaped like a chalice.

The plant appeared in Yemen early in the 13th century, perhaps from Ethiopia. It is a bush that grows from two to four metres high and thrives on altitude. Its fine leaves contain alkaloids that stimulate the sympathetic nerve. Scientific research concerning the effects of *qat* on the organism is being carried out at Sana'a University but is still embryonic.

One thing is certain: the heavy use of *qat* causes economic problems. For example, one can only grow this bush at the same altitude as coffee, an export product. Every year hectares of coffee plantations are replaced by *qat*. The government is aware of the situation, and in the last ten years has put a high tax on its sale.

The most appreciated variety grows right around Taiz on the mountainsides. And here I am chewing the best *qat* in Yemen, probably in the world. Yet I don't feel a thing and don't really like the taste. Abdullah seems to be in the seventh heaven. An oversize wad as big as a tangerine gives a clown-like air to a normally harmonious face. I can't help asking my M.P. friend if it's wise to drive on these dangerous roads after consuming so much *qat*. He assures me that, on the contrary, Abdullah will see better and have faster reflexes than usual. *Inch a Allah*! The masons who build the high

Boy wearing a striped turban. →

90

minarets, a very dangerous job, are great *qat* consumers, and this is said to add to their dexterity.

Toward the end of the afternoon we take the return road to Sana'a. Four hours and a half of fear and trembling... especially after nightfall when the powerful truck lights blind us brutally in the sharp curves. Abdullah has a rather jerky but sure touch on the steering wheel. Sitting beside him, young Hassan tears more leaves off his bouquet of *qat* and stuffs them delicately into our dear driver's mouth, which already holds such a massive wad that one fears his cheek will burst.

If we had had time we would have returned by the route of the Tihama along the Red Sea coast, a long strip 30 to 60 kilometres wide, a semi-desert plain that already reminds one of Africa. The small mud dwellings or the straw huts on a frame of branches, round or rectangular in form and well-adapted to the torrid climate, are plastered on the inside. People often sleep in the open on beds of woven rope.

At a hundred or so kilometres from Taiz on the Red Sea is a little, run-down port, Mokha, which has a dream quality for nostalgic visitors. Like Timbuktu, Katmandu, Singapore, Bali, Belem... Between the 17th and 19th centuries Mokha was a veritable metropolis, exporting dates, myrhh and frankincence, and a renowned variety of coffee grown on the heights of Yemen.

In the 16th century, when Europe and the Ottoman empire were discovering the delights of coffee, Mokha was the only source of supply, and remained so until the British introduced it to Ceylon (now Sri Lanka), and the Dutch to Indonesia. The arrival of the British in Aden in 1839 marked Mokha's decline. Its name was reduced to that of a variety of coffee, and the city to a small town of 10,000 inhabitants living mainly from fishing, in the midst of the ruins of a prestigious past—a few facades of rich merchants' villas.

From Mokha one can follow the coast northward and find long beaches fringed with palm trees. Those of Al-Khuawkhah, the finest beaches in Yemen, are worth the detour. In the next few years the government will make this the site of a large hotel complex, or a tourist village.

A peasant from the Tihama. →

On the road we pass through peaceful villages like hundreds more in the Tihama. Once a week, on market day, they spring suddenly to life, invaded by the inhabitants of neighbouring villages who come to sell their goods: basketwork, pottery, fruits and vegetables. The population is hospitable and the women—very beautiful—are not veiled. The men wear a *fouta*, a white shirt and a curious, wide-brimmed hat.

The best road for going from Taiz to Hodeida (Yemen's biggest port) passes through the interior, permitting a stop at Zabid, another jewel of Yemenite architecture. Its superb brick houses, whitewashed with gypsum, often have a beautiful interior courtyard. In the early 9th century Zabid was the capital of a kingdom founded by Muhammad bin Ziad, an erudite man of letters. He transformed his capital into a vast university which for a long time was one of the great centres of Islamic culture.

Hodeida began to develop in the mid-19th century during the second Turkish occupation, but it was not until this century that it became a modern port, the "gate to Yemen", and a city of 155,000 inhabitants. A young city, Hodeida has little attraction for history and architecture buffs.

Here, as elsewhere in the Third World, there are police barricades at the entrances and exits of cities. Gendarmes stop vehicles, check papers and examine the contents of trucks in search of contraband goods. But Abdullah is unperturbed by police barricades: his official licence plate, he is sure, should take care of these petty nuisances. Indeed, the barriers seem to inspire him. Not only does he not slow down, he accelerates, passing the line of vehicles on the right, honking furiously and yelling guttural insults at anyone, military or civilian, who seems not to appreciate his carefree style. It seems that everyone knows Abdullah, everybody loves him. He had already honked and shouted his way along this stretch in the Imam's day.

Dead-tired but happy, we arrive in Sana'a. I would have been sorry to die *before* seeing Taiz...

CHAPTER V

ROWDHA, THULA AND THE YEMEN OF TODAY

*If you are different from me,
my brother, you take nothing
from me: you enrich my life.*

Antoine de Saint-Exupéry

The traveller, whether he stays a week (not enough!) or a month in Yemen, often takes Sana'a as his base, from which he can make excursions to the main sites of interest in the country and, in most cases, get back to his hotel the same day.

Today, for example, I have decided to take a rest from the beauties of Sana'a and spend a few hours in the village of Rowdha, about twenty kilometres return.

Rowdha means "garden" in Arabic. For the time being a misnomer here! The season has been dry and this garden town looks more like a desert. The arable land appears stony, with only a few dusty bushes defying the drought. But at the summer's end Rowdha produces the best and sweetest grapes in the country. Only a few years ago the vineyards were irrigated from wells where dromedaries or donkeys helped to draw the water. The apparatus is still there, but now plastic pipes, that need fear no frost, slink through the streets bringing water to houses and gardens.

Apart from this visible plumbing, is there anything in Rowdha to tell us we are in the 20th century and not 1,000 B.C.? Not very much, indeed. Here and there a stretch of electric wire, or, on the roof of a rich man's house, against the blue sky, the etched lines of a TV antenna. And amid the rubbish in the street, empty plastic containers—alas, not biodegradable.

On arriving in Rowdha we quickly dispensed with the car and decided to walk. A bit of a street, a little square, an alleyway, a world, the end of the world. Swarms of children among the goats, the chickens, the dogs, the

Agriculture, traditional style, near Thula. →

cats. They play with anything and nothing, like children everywhere. A little boy is rolling a tire worn to the cord, making a noise like a truck with a broken muffler. The end of the world? Well... We spy the carcass of a 1949 Chevrolet, stripped of everything that was strippable. What is left is a vague, rusted shape, thank goodness biodegradable. In a thousand years the Chevy may have turned into beneficial dust, a little iron to help make children's muscles grow, recuperated via spinach...

Yes, the end of the world. But not all the children are playing. A little girl, her face too pale, her skirt too long, emerges from an impressive red-stone house, with a small pail of green plastic. Without a second's hesitation she picks out a she-goat, ties her up and milks the pail brimming full. A child who is not playing, who is doing something very important.

The dusty streets of Rowdha are lined with magnificent houses— Yemenite architecture always asserts its rights—with trees as ancient as Arabia, centuries-old mosques, including the Great Mosque built by Ahmad ibn al-Qasim (1676-1681), a square surrounded by four galleries of colonnades, dominated by a round minaret, decorated with Surahs from the Koran carved into the stone.

Not far from the mosque is the Imam's former palace, now an inn; but it has remained a gem of Yemen's architecture. From its terrace the view of Rowdha is fantastic: the houses that are not palaces could well *be* palaces.

From house to house, never quite the same lines, colours, whims or arabesques. In the coloured-glass windows we are surprised to find the star of Zion: the great specialists of this very Yemenite handicraft were, for a long time, the Jews.

Back in Sana'a I meet with university people, politicians, businessmen, who teach me much about the country over a coffee or a *qishr*. They have trouble talking about one Yemen without alluding to the other, or without dreaming of the day when Greater Yemen will exist again. For the moment the two states continue on their parallel paths, united by a common faith, culture and history, but separated by their ideology.

After the revolution of 1962, North Yemen (that is, the Yemen Arab Republic) showed its difference from the imams' régime by its generous openness to the world and its frank cooperation with the Eastern and Western

The smile of a child. →

98

countries. In contrast, South Yemen (the People's Democratic Republic of Yemen) chose the socialist path, a socialism tempered by Islamic values to be sure. In recent years, without disavowing its Marxist ideology or its friendship with the Soviets, South Yemen has moved closer to the capitalist Arab countries like the United Arab Emirates, Kuwait and Saudi Arabia, who contribute effectively to its economic development.

From 1962 to 1978 North Yemen has had its ups and downs, politically and economically. The first president of the republic, Abdullah al-Sallal, was deposed in 1967 and replaced by Abd al-Rahman al-Iryani. Following a coup d'État in 1974 Ibrahim al-Hamdi acceded to the presidency. In 1977 al-Hamdi was assassinated, as was his successor Ahmad al-Ghashmi a year later.

Observers were beginning to think that Yemen was ungovernable and that the expectations aroused by the revolution of 1962 would never be realized. But in a single decade the fifth president, Ali Abdullah Saleh, was to transform the country and at last give it a stable régime, open to progress and ready to cure Yemen of its chronic under-development. He established excellent relations with Saudi Arabia and all the other Arab countries, as well as those of the Eastern and Western blocs, but without aligning himself with either camp. He reorganized the army and put down the rebellion of the National Democratic Front. He maintains good relations with South Yemen and is continuing to negotiate the project of re-unification. Finally, president Saleh has held democratic elections, which previous presidents had promised but failed to do. For the first time in Yemen's history, in July, 1988, a parliament of 159 members was elected by universal suffrage.

One of the régime's important achievements will certainly remain that it restored the confidence of the international community, whose economic cooperation is essential to the country's development. Its economic problems were dangerously aggravated in recent years, partly because of the recession which even affected the rich Arab oil-producing countries, with the result that their financial aid to Yemen was reduced, as was their need for migrant workers from Yemen—the latter a very important source of foreign currency.

Finally, in July, 1984, came some good news that might transform Yemen's future by speeding up its economic recovery: the Hunt Oil Company of Texas had discovered a large oil field north-east of Sana'a. It is expected that its production will supply local needs and leave a large surplus for

An unusual house on the Thula road. →

export. This black gold will help to consolidate the foundation of the young republic economically and politically by ensuring a certain independence in relation to the oil-producing Arab countries.

What strikes the visitor is the enthusiasm of the Yemenites in attacking, on all fronts simultaneously, the enormous task of bringing their country in a few years out of the Middle Ages and into the 20th century.

There remains, of course, a great deal to do. But we must remember that only yesterday Yemen was one of the most isolated countries in the world, and one of the least developed. A country practically without schools or—until 1970—a university, so that it could count on only a tiny group of people to solve a multitude of problems. It was a country with no qualified administrators, no engineers, no doctors, no national currency, no banking system, almost no electricity, no aqueducts, no highway system, no industry, no skilled workers and no agriculture apart from food crops.

What Yemen has already accomplished in record time is a kind of miracle that should capture the admiration of the rich countries of the world and convince them to take part more generously in the development of this admirable country.

An interesting phenomenon is the activity of the Yemen Development Associations, local organizations that carry out small projects in the villages: digging wells, improving irrigation, building roads, schools, aqueducts. Gathered into a national confederation, these associations are run by the peasants themselves. They have helped to solve the problem of drinking-water as well as water to irrigate the terraces surrounding the villages which are always perched high on the mountains. Water is scarce up there, but the lofty locations gave protection in the days of wars. The Development Associations are financed by the government, private donations and the members themselves.

This initiative is all the more opportune in that the population is mainly rural and lives in small villages that are often hard to get to. During a recent census some 50,000 villages were visited, inhabited by 85 per cent of Yemen's over ten million population. To these can be added about a million migrant workers. This is a considerable population for the Arabian peninsula.

A little girl, and Kawkaban. →

102

Thus it is urgent for Yemen to modernize its agriculture, which has always been its prime vocation. At high altitudes (between 1,300 and 3,000 metres), thanks to the terrace system, grain grows well: wheat, sorghum, barley, corn, not to mention potatoes, vegetables, fruits, *qat* and coffee. Lower down we find fig, almond and frankincense trees. Finally, in the lowlands of the Tihama with their tropical climate, cotton, dates and various tropical fruits are produced in addition to cereals.

During the last ten or fifteen years the main cities (Sana'a, Hodeida, Taiz, Sa'da, Marib) have developed very fast, their populations soaring because of the rural exodus, the arrival of South Yemenites who disagree with the Marxist régime, and the tendency of the migrant workers, on their return, to settle in the cities rather than in their villages of origin. In the same period the number of trucks, buses and private cars has increased enormously, complicating traffic problems and requiring the rapid extension of the road system—a very costly venture in a mountainous country.

Another phenomenon peculiar to Yemen is the massive exodus of the best workers, attracted by the high wages paid in rich neighbouring countries such as Saudi Arabia. It is true that the migrants bring in more foreign currency to Yemen than any other source. But these excellent workers are almost all ex-farmers who rarely go back to the farm. Formerly self-sufficient, Yemen has to import much of the food it consumes. And the new industries suffer from the scarcity of skilled local manpower.

In a very short time Yemen has gone through profound sociological changes. A few years ago the tribe, the village were the centre of a Yemenite's life. Economically, socially, politically and religiously, the tribe met its own needs. That was possible because Yemen, protected by the imams against foreign influences, remained a self-sufficient economic unit. But the Yemenite migrant workers were already bringing home from abroad new ideas and customs different from those of their tribes, and their higher standard of living prompted them to settle in the cities on their return. Their long absences from home contributed to the emancipation of the women, who now had an opportunity to prove themselves outside the household. Because of the scarcity of manpower we find them in growing numbers in offices and even in factories. The number of Yemenite students attending the big universities of the Arab world, Europe and America is also steadily increasing. The influence of radio and, now, television, the presence of Egyptian teachers and Chinese, Soviet, German and even American experts, and the arrival of

Fine example of a brick *shubbak*. →

a flood of foreign businessmen and tourists—all these factors tend to weaken the old Yemenite traditions. For better or for worse! Perhaps very little time remains for observing the last civilized country in the world emerging from the Middle Ages...

Sana'a, on a Friday. This is the Moslem Sunday. No one works, people go to the mosque to pray, the main family meal is a little more elaborate than usual. Yemenite generally work from 8:00 a.m. to 2:00 p.m., and as their week-end has only one day they actually work 36 hours a week, just as we do.

For the Friday family lunch, the equivalent of our Sunday dinner, I have been invited by a businessman, a friend of friends, who also looks more like a prince from the Thousand and One Nights than like an importer of wheat and flour.

Another beautiful Yemenite house in brownstone, with low doorways and massive granite stairways. On the first floor up, we find ourselves in the *mafraj* or reception room, we sit on soft cushions placed along the walls. Before entering we remove our shoes, and no doubt we would be more at home if we wore the *fouta*, the Yemenite loincloth. We are served a very spicy lamb bouillon, in which I detect the taste of caraway. Then we are taken to another room, the centre of which is covered by some thirty dishes placed on the floor on a plastic tablecloth. There are about twenty of us, including three male children. The menu is traditional with a few variants: crêpes softened by a curdled-milk sauce; cream of chick-peas; minced meat with hard-boiled eggs; stuffed peppers and tomatoes; potatoes; saffron rice; roast lamb; lamb "au jus"; a large, sweet pie brushed with honey; onion, tomato and cucumber salads; two kinds of unleavened bread; and, to finish off, a much-loved Yemenite specialty called *saltah*: a sauce of a beautiful green colour, with a bitter taste, brought in simmering in a great iron pot.

Seated on the floor, we eat with the right hand as is commonly done in Africa and Asia. A third of humanity eats with its hands, another third with sticks, which leaves the users of knives and forks in a minority.

On the occasion of a meal like this, a sort of gastronomic celebration, Yemenites eat an enormous amount, especially of lamb. When I refuse a fourth helping I feel that it grieves my hosts, who take advantage of the slightest inattention on my part to slip another tender morsel on my plate.

A mafraj and its stained glass. →

106

Back to the *mafraj* with its soft cushions, where plates of very red, refreshing watermelon await us. We end with a typical Yemen tea infused from the husks of coffee beans, flavoured with ginger or cardamom.

There were twenty of us. All male. If I hadn't risked an indiscreet glance into the kitchen, I might never have suspected that there was at least one young woman there who was probably responsible for preparing this excellent meal. Since the 1962 revolution the situation of Yemenite women has distinctly improved, and the present government is in the process of liberalizing it further, especially insofar as access to education and management positions is concerned. The resistance comes from the families themselves, which remain strongly attached to traditional values.

Our host brings an incense burner. Threads of blue smoke curl upward. We breathe in the perfume and pass the lovely ceramic object on to our neighbour. Soon our host returns, this time with a bottle of perfume to be sprinkled on our hands and clothes. I manage to read the label: *Derby*, by Guerlain, Paris.

When I have an hour to spare between meetings, I stroll at random through my neighbourhood. A nearby street is closed to traffic and reserved for the small merchants who stay late into the night with their displays. One finds the same things for sale as in the bazaars: small plastic items, bar soap, toothpaste, socks, undergarments, shirts etc. Discount merchandise made in Singapore, China, Korea. At nearly every street corner there is a small vendor whose whole stock is a pile of raisins on an outspread newspaper, or a few packs of cigarettes with two or three chocolate bars. But in the larger streets one is astonished by the impressive numbers of shops abounding in the most sophisticated electronic equipment, or perfume shops filled with the best French products. In Yemen, men are as enthusiastic about perfume as women are.

Every walk in Sana'a is an adventure. This evening, in the heart of the city, I strolled along beside an interminable wall with no idea what lay behind it, until I came to a door that opened on a vast cemetery of striking austerity. As far as the eye could see there were gravestones, all alike and barely distinguishable from the rocky ground. The moonlight fell ash-silver on this field of desolation. Not a single flower or shrub, no monuments, no inscriptions on the slabs. The Prophet states that Allah will bless those who

Old man in Shibam. →

are buried anonymously. Here and there, silent phantoms move, dark and blurred: women searching for a husband's grave.

Lunch at the home of my friend the politician. In a suburb of Sana'a, an immense house, or rather several houses linked by interior courtyards and surrounded by deep gardens where irrigation has coaxed along a fine vineyard, some pomegrenade trees and, of course, *qat*.

As in all Yemenite houses, shoes are removed before one enters a carpeted room. A classic *mafraj*, with big windows and stained-glass fanlights, arabesques carved in the plaster, gold-lettered verses from the Koran as reminders of the presence of God. But this is a wealthy home, and everything is more elaborate, larger, more refined. The menu is not unlike yesterday's, but the plates are more attractive, the service is more efficient and the lamb— do I imagine it?—seems more tender. As a supreme refinement, our host offers a *fouta* to everyone wearing pants, which are not very comfortable if one is to spend hours sitting cross-legged on the floor. The *fouta* is a single, rectangular piece of cotton, generally in a checked pattern, sewed in a large circle and pulled tight arount the waist, falling half-way down the legs. Right away one feels lighter and better disposed to enjoy the comfortable cushions. This very practical garment is popular throughout Asia. It's the *dhoti* of Sri Lanka, the *sarong* of South-East Asia. The Yemenites are wearing European jackets and shirts, and their headgear is often a turban, the shape, colour and cloth of which are infinitely varied. A wide sash in cloth of gold or silver holds the *jambias*, the most modest of which cost at least $25 U.S., while the rich wear daggers worth thousands of dollars. The usual sheath is of green cord, but the best are in finely-chased solid silver. The grip is made of horn, often translucid with a gold or silver piece attached on each side. A *jambia* is passed from father to son as an heirloom.

In the home, where they spend most of their time, the women wear an ample dress with long sleeves. The skirt is long enough to hide the calves. In the presence of a male visitor they cover their head with a shawl drawn across the face to hide all but their eyes. In the street, where they rarely go, they literally wrap themselves in a large, brilliantly coloured cloth. In the cities women often wear a kind of black sack-dress of silk or rayon, the *sharshaf*, of Egyptian origin.

With a docile Abdullah, no doubt in a state of grace due to a healthy ration of *qat*, we will go off today to discover yet another wonder of this

A street in Sana'a. →

110

country, which has an endless supply of them: the little town of Thula, located an hour's drive from Sana'a. The road is good, but there is plenty of excitement in the first quarter-hour as we zigzag through high mountains before reaching a plateau: fields of dry grasses here and there, in a rocky, almost lunar immensity. Soon the rainy season will add patches of green to this landscape, where everything now is a harmony in ochre: mountains, fields, rocks, pebbles and even the dusty-coated donkeys and dromedaries. Perched on the mountainsides, the villages with their heavy stone houses blend into the scene.

The plateau suddenly dips and we find ourselves in a kind of Grand Canyon lacking only the camera-laden tourists. All at once Abdullah emits a few raucous but joyous sounds and points at Mount Thula, a huge peak rising like a dream-fortress. It is crowned by an ancient red stronghold around the feet of which lies the little town of Thula, a pure jewel of Yemenite architecture. Abdullah drives inside the walls onto a small square beyond which the car cannot go. We have a feeling that he has often been here with other visitors and has no real desire to guide us through the maze of streets so narrow that in places one can almost touch the houses on both sides. He seems to be telling us that there are guides for that, and that he wouldn't mind a rest. He opens the trunk of the car, where there is a small mattress, made to measure for him. The trunk is his personal *mafraj*, with cushions, a supply of cigarettes, mineral water and a very large bouquet of *qat*.

Abdullah is right: why should we deprive young Ibrahim of his living? He offers his services in very correct Engligh. Our dear Abdullah speaks only Arabic, which always prevents his enthusiastic explanations from getting through to us. Ibrahim is perhaps twenty five, with a young, somewhat sad face and a scrawny beard.

To tell thè truth, I wouldn't mind doing without a guide. I'd like to lose myself in the labyrinth of Thula and dream the magic of this millenary place, the enormous stone houses several storeys high, piled side by side but never quite touching, so that light can enter on all sides. Sometimes the houses are linked by a little covered bridge, also of stone, a hyphen between two homes, thus adapted in order to lodge the extended family that may have as many as sixty members.

The peak of Thula. →

112

The kind of impression Thula made on me—a real heart-throb—has struck me a few times before in my life when I was confronted by some marvel of architecture, some place where man has succeeded in surpassing himself: the temples at Angkor, the Taj Mahal, Egypt's pyramids, Machu-picchu... But in all those cases I was expecting the shock, whereas I expected nothing of Thula, a name I had never heard. My emotion perhaps came from the fact that this is no phantom monument inhabited by legend but deserted by man. Thula has never ceased to live, it is still vibrant with the joys and sorrows of its several thousand inhabitants, among them Ibrahim, a descendant of those who built this masterpiece.

A powerful impression of being in a science-fiction film. The time-warp takes me back five, ten centuries, to a town that has remained intact, with its surrounding wall, its deep cistern which gathers rainwater, its large, round stones, flat and sculpted so as to grind grain for flour; its superb palace, the local residence of the Imam and still lived-in by one of his many sons until the revolution of 1962; its souk with shops so small that the merchants can not stand upright but spend the day seated in front of their little baskets of ginger, cumin, raisins and coffee-bean husks. To make more room for merchandise a vendor has made a niche in the wall large enough to accommodate his hookah, its long yellow tube snaking between the baskets to his mouth.

Thula's tortuous alleys are sometimes so narrow that the sunlight never reaches the ground. They stay relatively cool even at mid-day. Some of these great houses seem uninhabited, though sometimes, through a low doorway, there appears a child with a timid smile.

"Of course they aren't empty," Ibrahim explains. "On the contrary, all these houses are teeming with people. But as we never use the ground floor, a kind of great hall that formerly housed the animals, it seems from the street as if nobody's there. For example look at this house, it appears completely calm. But there's smoke coming out from holes between the third-floor stones. That's the kitchen, away up there, and on the fifth floor, where you see all the coloured glass windows, that's the *mafraj*, a big room where maybe a dozen men are sitting, talking and chewing *qat*. There's a terrific view from up there."

The originality of Thula's architecture is that they do not use bricks for the upper storeys, as is done in Sana'a, but only hewn stone. The large

A street in Thula. →

114

windows are often paired and surmounted by an oculus, or linked by a semi-circular arch with petal-shaped openings.

The former palace of the Imam serves as an inn for the rare travellers who spend the night in Thula.

"What if we went up to the *mafraj* to see the view, if it's so splendid?"

Ibrahim smiles and leads the way up the palace's dark staircase. The steps are irregular and too high. We arrive at the top fairly winded. (It's not age, it's the altitude: Thula is more than 2,000 metres above the level of the Red Sea.) The effort is worthwhile. From a small terrace we can see almost the whole town, the old mosque, and Mount Thula, on which we perceive the movements of some intrepid souls who have scaled the peak. At the beginning of the 16th century the Turks invaded Yemen, but they never managed to conquer the fortress of Thula. Seen from our perch in the palace, we understand why.

This is the last day of our voyage to Yemen—a glimpse of earthly joy one would like to preserve forever. The extraordinary beauty of this country, the overwhelming majesty of its mountains, the golden light of its valleys, the mystery, the pride and the open-hearted hospitality of its inhabitants— all these things tempt one to come back some day...

In the uncertain light of my recollections, encumbered by as many memories "as if I were a thousand years old", Yemen will shine on like an incomparable diamond. With Flaubert, I want to exclaim: "There are places on earth so beautiful, you want to hug the globe to your heart!"

116

ADVICE TO TRAVELLERS

> *He who leaves will be torn by regrets, but he who stays will fall to pieces.*
>
> Paul Morand

Yemen has a great future as a destination for tourists. The government has been prompt to realize that tourism is a good source of foreign currency, which the country urgently needs. Accordingly, the Department of Information and Culture intends to develop tourist infrastructures over the next few years, while trying to avoid the damage to culture and the environment caused by tourists in other Third World countries.

Luckily, the mysterious attraction of distant Yemen appeals to an élite, the better kind of tourists, the ones who want to get away from the beaten path, who do not travel to the ends of the earth merely to bore themselves to death on a sandy beach they could find anywhere, who don't fall into a depression if they are deprived of golf, a shopping centre and assorted night clubs. Yemen is the last resort for those who have seen everything but would still like to be "astonished" in Cocteau's sense. Eclectic travellers, fascinated by the mountain landscapes, exotic nights on the Red Sea, the nobility of an as yet unspoiled nature, the prodigious splendour of an architecture unique on earth, the vestiges of civilizations thousands of years old, barely explored even by archaeologists, and, most important of all, a population that has remained pure and proud, only recently in contact with the outside world, but hospitable, open and generous.

Passport and Visa

Foreign visitors must have a passport valid for at least three months, and a visa issued by an embassy or consulate of the Yemen Arab Republic. They must fill out a form (2 copies) and provide 2 passport-format photos.

Stained glass in Yemenite houses. →

Cost of the visa: about $30 U.S. Yemen refuses to issue visas to those who have an Israeli or South African passport, or whose passport contains a visa for either of those countries.

A visitor's visa is valid for one month. Those who want to stay longer in Yemen can obtain an extension of their visa from the Immigration Office. A few days before leaving the country they must also obtain an exit visa.

Diplomatic representatives of Yemen in the world

Arab Organizations

P.O. Box 926989
Amman, Jordan
Tel.: 668604 — 668338

Jadiriya 923/28/29

Baghdad, Iraq
Tel.: (1) 776-0647/776-0648/
776-0649

Algeria

74 rue Bouraba
Algiers
Tel.: 797400/798197

Canada

Consulate
56 Sparks Street, Suite 500
Ottawa, Ontario K1P 5A9
Tel.: (613) 230-6136

China

4 Dongzhi Men Wai Dajie
Beijing
Tel.: 523346

Czechoslovakia

Washingtonova 17
12522 Prague 1
Tel.: (2)222411

Djibouti

P.O. Box 1913
127/4 Ahmad Ibrahim Building
Djibouti
Tel.: 352975/352976

East Germany

Waldstrasse 15
1110 — Berlin
Tel.: 4800391

Egypt

28, Ameen El-Rafai Street,
Dokki Cairo
Tel.: 3484375

Ethiopia

P.O. Box 664
Addis Ababa
Tel.: 181265/181260

France

21, avenue Charles Floquet
75007 — Paris
Tel.: (1)43-06-66-22

India

B-55 Pashami Marg, Vassant
Vihar
New Delhi 110057
Tel.: (11)674064

Iraq

Jadiriya 923/28/29
Baghdad
Tel.: 776-0647

Iran

Bucharest Ave. No. 26
Teheran
Tel.: 628011

Italy

Via Verona 3
00161 Roma
Tel.: (06)4270811

Japan

8th Floor, Room 807, No. 38
Kowa Bldg.
12-24, Nishi Azabu 4-Chome
Minato-Ku
Tokyo
Tel.: (03)499-7151

Jordan

P.O. Box 3085
Jabal Amman, Third Floor
Zabram St.
Amman
Tel.: 642382 — 642381

Merchant in the market. →

Kuwait

P.O. Box 4626
13047 Safat
Rawdah, Block 3
Yousef as-Sabih St,
Villa 15
Kuwait City
Tel.: 2518827

Lebanon

Blvd Khaldé-Quzai
Imm. Ingénieur Ryad Amaiche
Beirut
Tel.: 805341/2

Libya

P.O. Box 4839
Sharia Ubei ben Ka'ab 36
Tripoli
Tel.: 32323

Morocco

11, rue Abou-Hanifa Agdal
Rabat
Tel.: 74363

Netherlands

Surinamestraat 9
2585 GG The Hague
Tel.: (070)65-39-36

Oman

P.O. Box 3701
16, Algarm, Villa 52
Muscat
Tel.: 696966

Pakistan

46, St 12
F-6/3
Islamabad
Tel.: (51)821146

Qatar

Villa Mohammad' Maayouf
Al-Naimy
Doha
Tel.: 671050/671051

Saudi Arabia

P.O. Box 94356
Riyadh 11693
Tel.: (1)464-2077

Somalia

P.O. Box 264
Via Martyr Mahamoud Harbi
Mogadishu
Tel.: 80310

Sudan

P.O. Box 1010
St 35, New Extension
Khartoum
Tel.: 43918/80310

Switzerland

Kistlerweg 2
3006 Berne
Tel.: (031)444885

Syria

Abou Roumaneh
Charkassieh
Damascus
Tel.: 335643/339807/244427

Tunisia

50 rue Mouaouia ibn Soufiane
al-Menzah 6
Tunis
Tel.: 237-933

United Arab Emirates

P.O. Box 2095
Abu Dhabi
Tel.: 829825/822800

United Kingdom

41, South Street
London W1
Tel.: 629 9905/6/7/8

United Nations

747 Third Avenue, 8th Floor
New York, N.Y. 10017 U.S.A.
Tel.: (212) 3551730/3551731

U.S.A.

600 New Hampshire Ave., N.W.
Suite 840
Washington DC 20037
Tel.: (202) 965-4760
     (202) 965-4761
     (202) 965-4781
     (202) 965-4785
     (202) 965-4786

U.S.S.R.

2 Neopalimovskii Per 6
Moscow
Tel.: 2461814/2464427/2461554

West Germany

Godesberger Allee 125-127
5300 — Bonn
Tel.: 0228-376851/2/3/4

Taharir Square in Sana'a. →

Foreign diplomatic representatives in Sana'a

Algeria

P.O. Box 509
Ring Road
Tel.: (2) 247755

China

Az-Zubairy St.
Tel.: (2)275340

Czechoslovakia

P.O. Box 2501
Safiya Road
Tel.: (2)247946

East Germany

P.O. Box 15
26th September St.
Tel.: (2)270065

Ethiopia

P.O. Box 234
Az-Zubairy St.
Tel.: (2) 72825

France

P.O. Box 1286
Al-Bounia
Tel.: (2)73196

India

P.O. Box 1154
Off Az-Subairy St.
Tel.: (2)241980

Iraq

P.O. Box 498
South Airport Rd
Tel.: (2)244122

Iran

P.O. Box 1437
Hadda Rd.
Tel.: (2)206945

Italy

P.O. Box 1152
65 Gamal Abd an-Nasser St.
Tel.: (2)72792

Japan

P.O. Box 817
Ring Road
West Safiya
Tel.: (2)207356

Jordan

P.O. Box 2152
Customs Lane
As-Safiya
Tel.: (2)241794

Korea

P.O. Box 1234
Qiyada St.
Tel.: (2) 223504

Kuwait

P.O. Box 17036
Hadda Rd
Tel.: (2)208086

Lebanon

P.O. Box 2283
Hadda Rd.
Tel.: (2)240437

Libya

P.O. Box 1506
Ring Rd.
Tel.: (2) 272202/272203/272204

Netherlands

P.O. Box 463
Hadda Rd.
Tel.: (2)215626

Oman

P.O. Box 105
Hadda Rd.
Tel.: (2)72313

Pakistan

P.O. Box 2848
Ring Road
Tel.: (2)248812

Saudi Arabia

P.O. Box 1184
Zuhra House
Hadda Rd
Tel.: (2)240429

Somalia

P.O. Box 101
Hadda Rd
Tel.: (2)247842

Sudan

P.O. Box 517
Hadda Rd.
Tel.: (2)241811

Syria

P.O. Box 494
Hadda Rd.
Tel.: (2)247750

United Arab Emirates

P.O. Box 2250
Hadda Rd.
Tel.: (2)248777

United Kingdom

P.O. Box 1287
Hadda Rd
Tel.: (2)215630

U.S.A.

P.O. Box 1088
Beit Al-Halali Building
Tel.: (2)271950

U.S.S.R.

P.O. Box 1087
26 September St.
Tel.: (2)72353

West Germany

P.O. Box 2562
Outer Ring Rd
West Hadaa
Tel.: (2)72818

Little girl selling water melons. →

Customs

You may enter Yemen with 200 cigarettes or 250 grams of tobacco, or 50 cigars. Unless the traveller is a Moslem, he or she may also bring in duty-free one litre of alcoholic beverages. (No alcohol is sold in Yemen, and only a few big hotels are authorized to serve it to non-Moslem customers.) No duty is applied to gifts if their value does not exceed $25 U.S.

Under certain conditions (ask the consul), business people may bring in samples, brochures about their products, and audio-visual material.

Money

Yemen's money unit is the *riyal*. In the big hotels, American dollars or other hard currencies are accepted, as well as travellers' cheques and the main credit cards. Outside the larger cities or for bargaining in the souks it is better to have riyals.

Banks are open every day from 8:00 a.m. to noon, except on Fridays.

The Tourist Office

A government agency, the General Tourism Corporation is at the service of tourists and visitors. Its offices are located in the Maidan Attahrir, Sana'a, P.O. Box 129. Phone 76697 or 73935. Telex: 2592GTCORPYE. There are regional offices in Taiz, Hodeida and Ibb.

The Yemen Tourism Company

A para-governmental organization, unusual in that it was established in 1981 following an agreement between North Yemen and South Yemen with the goal of promoting tourism between the two countries, and between foreign countries and the two Yemens.

The Yemen Tourism Company provides all the services of a large travel agency, including the organization of group expeditions and trips. (Address: P.O. Box 1526, Sana'a, Yemen Arab Republic. Phone: 240372 or 79539. Telex: 2498 YEMTORYE.)

The principal cities have a number of good private travel agencies.

Airports

The Sana'a airport is located 15 kilometres from the city centre. On arrival you can change money at the airport. If you do not, you will have to make the taxi wait at the hotel entrance while the hotel cashier changes a traveller's cheque for you.

When leaving Sana'a, be sure you have enough riyals in your pocket to pay the airport tax. And of course you will not have forgotten to have a travel agency reconfirm your return flight! *At least* 72 hours in advance.

Sana'a is linked by direct flights to the big cities of Europe such as London, Paris, Frankfurt and Rome, and to a number of cities in Africa and Asia. *Yemenia* is the national airline, but several international lines fly to Sana'a.

Hodeida and Taiz also have international airports.

Woman in Yemenite dress. →

126

The climate

Because of its altitude, Yemen enjoys a temperate climate in most of the country, except on the coast of the Red Sea, which is tropical. Most of the historic sites that attract visitors are on the high plateaus or in the mountains. The climate of Sana'a is always pleasant. In winter, however, the temperature may go down near zero at night and, in summer, rise to 25° by midday.

Here are the average temperatures of the three main cities, in degrees Celsius:

	September (minimum)	March (maximum)	April (minimum)	August (maximum)
SANA'A	8	16	16	26
TAIZ	12	20	22	29
HODEIDA	25	32	30	45

Clothing

Men should wear a light-weight suit, in dark colours for receptions or official meetings when shirt and tie are called for.

At all other times, a sport shirt and light pants or a bush shirt will do. Don't wear shorts or Bermudas. A sweater is necessary in the evening in cities at higher altitudes, especially in winter.

A good pair of walking shoes is indispensable. Yemen is a paradise for mountain hiking and sightseeing on foot. (This is how villages and markets should be visited.)

Even in the mountains, where the air is cold, don't trust the sun. Use sun-screen on exposed skin and wear a hat.

Women should dress very modestly if they want to avoid shocking their hosts: skirts as long as possible, an ample blouse, not low-cut, covering shoulders and preferably arms. Outside the cities they would do well to wear a scarf on their heads.

Why risk offending men and women who welcome us in *their country*, just for a vestimentary whim? The Yemenites are not benighted just because they have preserved certain habits of modesty that were our own not so many years ago...

Rules of hygiene

By and large, Yemen has a healthy climate; but like in other countries in tropical latitudes the foreign visitor must take a minimum of precautions that will ensure an agreeable visit with no health problems.

At least two months before departure consult a specialized clinic which will work out a vaccination program for you, prescribe medication against malaria and give you basic advice. Here are some rules which apply not only to visitors to Yemen but to all travellers in tropical lands. I borrowed them, in fact, from a book I published a few years ago (*Travelling in Tropical Countries*, Hurtig Publishing, Edmonton, 1985).

A shopkeeper in Sana'a. →

1.   The first day, on arriving in a tropical country, rest, and resist the temptation to set off in conquest of the new city. If you have crossed a good number of time zones, by no means schedule any immediate business or other meetings: you risk making bad decisions.

2.   For the first few days avoid exposure to the sun, heavy exercise, alcohol and overeating.

3.   Diarrhea can be brought on by overconsumption of iced drinks, alcohol and fruit.

4.   To counteract the effects of excessive perspiration (weakness, nausea, headache), particularly in the early part of your journey, you should take lots of liquids—boiled water, tea, coffee, carbonated beverages, beer. Drink to the point where your urine is almost colourless. Make a notable increase in your intake of table salt.

5.   You may feel unusually nervous and irritable for the first few days because of the fatigue brought on by the long air journey, the brusque change in climate, excessive perspiration, and sometimes diarrhea. The shock of a new environment and a radical change in routine can sometimes affect your outlook. Forewarned is forearmed against this transition period.

6.   Water. Copious amounts of liquids should be consumed in tropical countries, but this liquid intake must be clean. You are often told that the water in this hotel or that city is drinkable. That might well be for local people, but practically never for a foreigner with a different intestinal flora.

Volunteers who stay for several years in the same country often end up by "getting used to the water." In fact, it is their intestinal flora that changes, which does not make them immune to water-borne disease. If you are in one or several countries for relatively short stays, drink only water that has been held at a brisk boil for three to five minutes. In Yemen, by the way, one finds excellent mineral waters everywhere.

Take absolutely no ice-cubes or any beverage made with unboiled water, and remember that certain fruit juices may be "stretched" with untreated water.

Don't trust the thermos jug of ice water brought to your room. Of course you will be told it is drinkable, but even if it were, it wouldn't be for long unless the thermos itself had been sterilized.

Naturally you should brush your teeth only with boiled water or bottled mineral water.

7.   Fresh vegetables. As a general rule, eat only cooked vegetables. Eat absolutely no lettuce or other raw, unpeeled vegetables. They often cause intestinal disease.

8.   Fresh fruit. Peel all fruit (including tomatoes) after giving your hands a thorough washing.

9.   Dairy products. They are scarce in tropical countries and rarely pasteurized. Best to avoid milk, butter, cheese and ice cream. Make do with powdered milk or boiled milk.

10.   Meat and fish. Eat only well-cooked meat and fish. Don't ever eat raw shellfish and be wary even of cooked ones. They could have been out in the sun too long beforehand.

11.   Restaurants. Don't ever succumb to the lure of a quaint little greasy spoon, especially if it is abuzz with flies; there will be ten times as many in the kitchen.

In Sana'a all the doors are blue... →

Hotels and restaurants

In a country that has been practically closed to foreign visitors until 1970, we mustn't expect to find as many hotels and restaurants as elsewhere in the world. However, in recent years the government of Yemen has made great efforts to provide the main tourist centres with modern hotels, some of which belong to big international chains and deserve their five stars. Others, more modest, compensate by offering visitors grandiose landscapes and unbeatable views. In several cities, even small ones, we find inns or *funduqs*—sometimes former palaces of the imams or members of the royal family—transformed into very agreeable small hotels, with their dazzling architecture, such as the Al Rawda on the outskirts of Sana'a, or the Dar-al-Hamd in the city centre. A stay in these ancient palaces gives the traveller an opportunity to discover the traditional architecture from within and savour the charms of the *mafraj*, which is on the top floor, and from which the imams, always afraid of a plot against them, could at least see their enemies coming!

Here is a list of the main hotels:

City/town	Rating	Address	Telephone	Telex	P.O. Box
Sana'a (area code 02)					
Sheraton	*****	Dahr Himyaer	237800/8	222	2467
Taj Sheba	*****	All abdulmognl Street	272872	2552	773
Hadda	*****	Hadda Road, Hadda	215215	2227	999
Al Rawdah	***	Al Rawdah	340227	2498	1505
Dar al Hamd	***	Broaddasting Zone	203055	2270	2178
Al Ikwah	**	Saif bin Duyazan Street	272250	2350	344
Al Mokha	**	Ali Abdulmogni Street	272881	2298	593
Al Iskander	*	Al Qasr Street	272834		8269
Al anwar	*	Ali Abdulmogni Street	272843		830
Shaharah	*	Ali Abdulmogni Street	272844		1646
Al Khayam	*	Al Oasr Street	71795		1112
Arwa	*	Al Oasr Street	276102/3		1481
Al Zahra	*	Ali Abdulmogni Street	272651		204
Al Oasr		Al Oasr Street	272404		
Taiz (area code 04)					
Marib	***	Jabal Dabooa	210350	8848	5285
Tourist	***	Al Makha	333031	8848	8388
Al Ikwah	**	Jabal Dabooa	210395		5413
Plaza	**	26th September Street	220224	9829	8168
Al Ganad	**	Al Akaba Street	210929		6866
Tahrir Tower	**	Lower Tahrir Street	221483		6380
De Luxe	**	Gamal Street	226351		6476
Hodeidah (area code 03)					
Ambassador	***	Sana'a Street	231247/50	5625	3491
Bristol	***	Sana'a Street	239197	5617	4205

A grand hotel in Sana'a. →

Transportation

Though Yemen has no railway, it has a good bus and collective taxi service. These means of transport—not expensive—enable the visitor to make contact with the population in an interesting way. But buses and collective taxis are usually jammed full, each traveller bringing along tons of baggage: bundles, baskets, bags of rice, babies, live chickens, etc.

You don't need to bring chickens, but at least have with you a few emergency provisions: fruits, nuts, cookies, and, above all, a big bottle of mineral water. And a reserve of toilet paper.

Travellers who are impatient, delicate or lacking a sense of humour should avoid such trips. The others will have a lot of fun and will learn a great deal.

Excursions by taxi are not expensive, but as in other places where they don't have a metre it's best to agree on the price before you start.

I would not advise renting a car without a driver. You need the dexterity of a Yemenite chauffeur to make your way through the ticklish city traffic and the hairpin bends of the mountain roads. In case of an accident, a driver will avoid complications for you.

Organized tours

I am no lover of organized tours, but I recommend them in Yemen. There is an infinity of things to see, even in the most isolated parts of the country, but Yemen has barely started building up its tourist infrastructure. The Yemen Tourism Company and the main travel agencies have cross-country vehicles available which make it possible to leave the highway and cut across the desert to see some abandoned town that was formerly the capital of a great kingdom. The guide will give you the explanations in your own language without which you would never have guessed the interest of some Sabaean inscription. Finally, in a country not overly rich in hotels and good restaurants, you will be sure of getting proper accommodation and meals, or at a pinch, of having a picnic and sleeping in a beautiful tent on the shore of the Red Sea rather than a perhaps too rudimentary inn.

For travelling outside of Sana'a you need a permit which you can get through the travel agency. If you really want to travel on your own, these permits can be obtained from the General Tourism Corporation.

Photography

Travellers who like to take pictures—and who could resist it in a country as fabulous as Yemen?—must use discretion. Children love being photographed. But it's best to ask permission of an adult. All it takes is a smile. According to tradition one must not photograph women, but a Yemenite guide or friend will give you the right advice for the circumstances. It is prohibited to take pictures of military gatherings, port facilities, airports, barracks or prisons. To shoot film or video one must obtain a permit from the Information and Culture Department.

Holidays

Yemenites use the Moslem calendar instituted by Omar, Muhammad's second successor, 1,350 years ago. The year One corresponds to 622 A.D., the year in which the prophet fled from Mecca to Medina.

Children love the camera. →

134

The Moslem calendar is quite different from ours, but visiting foreigners may well not even suspect its existence, as Yemenites are familiar with the Gregorian calendar.

However, it is useful to know the dates of national or religious holidays and, in particular, the movable obligatory fast of Ramadan. It lasts a month, during which Yemenites do not eat, drink or smoke between sunrise and sunset, which considerably slows social and economic activities during the day. The month ends with three days of festivity, the Shawwal. Visitors must take this into account if they want to see businessmen, officials or politicians.

Here are the holidays with fixed dates:

May 1:   Labour Day.

September 26:   Anniversary of the 1962 revolution.

October 14:   Anniversary of the 1963 revolution.

Religious feast days are on different dates each year because of the Moslem calendar:

12 Rabi'a Awwal: Birth of the prophet Muhammad.

10 Dhul-Hajjah: Feast of the 'Aid Al-Adha' (5 days).

1 Shawwal: Feast of the 'Aid Al-Fitr' (4 days).

1 Muharram: Moslem New Year.

Working hours are:

● Government departments and civil service: 8:00 a.m. to 2:00 p.m.

● Banks: 8:00 a.m. to noon.

● Post office: 8:00 a.m. to 1:00 p.m. and 4:00 p.m. to 8:00 p.m.

● Offices and businesses: 8:00 a.m. to noon 7:00 p.m. and 4:00 p.m. to 7:00 p.m.

The language

Not everyone is gifted for languages, but anyone can learn a few Arabic words, at least the polite formulas.

In Yemen, English is the most-used foreign language—in hotels, government, the larger businesses and tourist agencies. The population as a whole speaks only Arabic, but human beings always manage to make themselves understood. If they really want to! It's hard work, everyone laughs a lot and draws lots of pictures. And finally they say many things to each other.

Here are a few polite phrases that will add to the good humour of your encounters in Yemen:

Greetings	English Equivalent	Literal Meaning
Assalamu alaikom	It has no equivalent in English. It is said by one person who meets another any time, day or night.	Peace be upon you.

A descendant of the Himyarites? →

Wa'alikom assalam	Reply to the above.	And upon you be peace.
Sabah al Khair	Good morning.	Morning of good fortune.
Sabah annour	Reply to the above.	Morning of light.
Masal Khair	Good evening.	Evening of good fortune.
Masan noor	Reply to the above.	Evening of light.
Ma'as salama	Good bye, bye-bye.	Go with peace.
Fi amanil-lah	Good bye, bye-bye.	Go in God's protection.
Kaif halukom?	How are you, how do you do, how are you keeping, how are things with you?	How is your state of health, how are your conditions?
Bikhair, ma li shi, followed by 'al hamdulil-lah'	Reply to the above.	In a good state, in good health, I have nothing to complain, followed by 'Praise be to God'.
Allah Yibarek	Blessings.	God's blessings.
Ashkurak, shukran	Thank you, thanks.	I thank you, thanks.
Ahsant	Well done.	Well done, you did it well. Also used to thank someone for doing you a favour.
Al'afu, 'afwan	Pardon, excuse me, I beg your pardon, don't mention it.	Pardon, excuse me. Also used in reply to someone who thanks you for something.
Ana mut-assif	I am sorry.	I am sorry.
La bas, ma fish Khawf	It doesn't matter, don't worry.	No worry, nothing to fear.
Ahlan wa sahlan	Welcome.	Find relatives and comfort.
I'mal ma'roof	Please do me a favour.	Do me a favour.
Fadhlan, min fadhlak	Please.	Please, if you please.
Kaif assihha? Kaif sihatukom?	How is your health?	How is your health?
Tayyiba, wa kaif sihhatukom?	Good, and how is your health?	Good, and how is your health?
La samaha Allah	God forbid.	God forbid.
In sha Allah	God willing.	God willing.
Ma sha Allah, Ya salam	Said to express admiration for something nicely done.	God desired it to be so. How nice.
Hajat Khidma?	Any service?	Any service?

(Extract from YEMENIA magazine)

Buying a hookah is an adventure. →

Shopping

It goes without saying that if you want to bargain in the markets (souks), it is preferable to take along a Yemenite guide or friend. He knows the prices, has mastered the art of haggling, and may even be a distant cousin of the merchant.

Tourists will be tempted to take home a handsome *jambia*. You buy it from the craftsman who makes it in the open in front of his shop. They are to be had at a wide range of prices: the run-of-the-mill specimens cost at least $25 U.S., while ancient or finely-wrought *jambias* may be worth $1,000 U.S. or more.

The Yemenite hookah is another interesting object. You have to buy each component of it from a different craftsman: the copper base, the stem of turned wood, the bowl of baked clay and the long, flexible tube covered with velvet.

One finds admirable old jewelry in silver or white metal: necklaces, bracelets, earrings. You have to trust the jeweler, or buy at a (higher) fixed price in the shops of the hotel or at the General Tourism Corporation which has a handicrafts counter.

Hospitality

One of the joys of Yemen is the generous hospitality, even of the poorest host. Peasants, shopkeepers, policemen will seize the slightest pretext for offering you a cup of tea.

One day my photographer, Marc Hébert, had the notion of taking some photos in old Sana'a in the very late evening. He realized fully that he was the only foreigner still out in the streets—a foreigner who was enjoying himself by photographing coloured windows lit from the inside! But everyone was kind to him, and occasionally someone offered him a tea or an herbal concoction. One Yemenite suddenly grew more insistent: Marc must absolutely come along to his place. With the help of volunteer interpreters, Marc finally got the idea: his would-be host was a gendarme, and "his place" was the police station! In old Sana'a people are used to foreigners taking snapshots, "but never at night!"

At the station the gendarme sat Marc down on a handsome rug and offered him a glass of tea before asking him questions. By the third tea the two men had become fast friends and the policeman finally issued him a real invitation to dine at "his place" the following evening!

As soon as you become friendly with a Yemenite there is every chance that he will do you the honours of his house and table—an extraordinary cultural and gastronomic experience.

Don't forget to take your shoes off as soon as you enter the house. Before the meal your host will show you to a wash basin where you wash your hands: people eat with their hands, and everybody serves himself from the common dishes placed on the floor, on a tablecloth. Always use your right hand. The left is reserved for a function having to do with personal hygiene.

Yemenite women never eat with the men, but it may happen that a foreign woman is invited. Generally she will be led to the women's quarters, where the men, of course, never set foot. An opportunity to see how the other half lives in this world of men.

In the *mafraj* one sits on cushions during the soup course and (after the meal) to drink coffee or tea. Take care not to point the soles of your feet at anyone—it's a serious breach of form. But whatever happens, your Yemenite hosts will not hold it against you. Their sense of hospitality is such that they will shut their eyes to any blunder by an innocent visitor.

Have a good voyage!

An old *jambia* in silver. →
Cistern of the Thula mosque. →

Printed by Marquis
in Montmagny (Québec) Canada
May 1989